TRUE PATRIOTISM

BY THE SAME AUTHOR

No Rusty Swords
VOL. I OF THE COLLECTED WORKS
(FONTANA LIBRARY)
The Way to Freedom
VOL. II OF THE COLLECTED WORKS
(FONTANA LIBRARY)
Act and Being
Christology
(FONTANA LIBRARY)
Sanctorum Communio

BOOKS ABOUT DIETRICH BONHOEFFER

Dietrich Bonhoeffer
by Eberhard Bethge
The Form of Christ in the World
by John Phillips
I Knew Dietrich Bonhoeffer
edited by Wolf-Dieter Zimmermann & Ronald Gregor Smith
World Come of Age
edited by Ronald Gregor Smith

True Patriotism

LETTERS, LECTURES AND NOTES
1939–45

FROM THE
COLLECTED WORKS OF

Dietrich Bonhoeffer

VOLUME III

EDITED AND INTRODUCED BY
EDWIN H. ROBERTSON

TRANSLATED BY
EDWIN H. ROBERTSON
AND JOHN BOWDEN

Harper and Row, Publishers

NEW YORK, EVANSTON, SAN FRANCISCO,

LONDON

Contents

INTRODUCTION

Introduction

There are several reasons why this third volume differs considerably from the earlier two. *No Rusty Swords* and *The Way to Freedom* aimed at giving to the English reader the essence of the four (now five) substantial volumes of the *Gesammelte Schriften* as collected by Eberhard Bethge. Instead of following his procedure of publishing volumes devoted to 'The Ecumenical Movement', 'The Church Struggle', 'Theology and the Church' and 'Sermons', the English volumes, using most of the material in these four volumes, arranged it in a different manner. The object was to follow the development of the mind of Dietrich Bonhoeffer. The material was arranged chronologically with this purpose. By linking passages from Bonhoeffer's papers and letters and putting them as far as necessary in the setting of events, it was hoped to illustrate his theology, his attitude to events, his assessment of the ethics of his time, his involvement in the new and rapidly evolving ecumenical movement, etc. The various subjects were not separated, but Bonhoeffer's point of view was followed as he advanced on a broad front and considered, or was compelled to consider, many themes. The one exception to this was a series of lectures on Christology, extracted from the papers, partly reconstructed and published under the title *Christology* (the American title is *Christ the Center*). But in these first two volumes the reader could follow the development of Bonhoeffer's mind, watch it respond to events, and then at the end of each section a sermon or lecture was printed which Bonhoeffer had delivered at that time. I personally found those utterances most revealing, because they showed how far he was prepared to go in public – which was usually quite a long way![1]

This third volume is one more attempt to give to the English reader the essence of the *Gesammelte Schriften*, and covers the period from the outbreak of the war until Bonhoeffer's death. Several things have made this volume different from the others.

Firstly, Eberhard Bethge's monumental biography has been published in English, which means that the importance of Bonhoeffer's papers can now be fully assessed. The biography has also made new material available, some of which I have used, even though it does not appear in the *Gesammelte Schriften*. The third volume is therefore much more colourful than the other two.

Secondly, the period covered by this third volume includes that of the famous or infamous *Letters and Papers from Prison*, which are Bonhoeffer's best-known writings. It was impossible to follow the development of his mind during the prison period without summarizing and making reference to much of this material. This and other material has already appeared in print, but it can still be said of this third volume that, like the other two, the greater part of the text has not till now been available in English.

Thirdly, the practice of ending each section with a sermon or statement which Bonhoeffer made in public has been discontinued, because he was not allowed to make statements in public during most of the period covered by this volume.

Fourthly, this volume covers the last years of his life. In both

---

[1] All material in these two volumes, except for certain exchanges of letters and certain public statements which were included for completeness, appeared in English for the first time.

the previous volumes it was possible to look forward, knowing that his mind would develop yet further. When we close this volume we have reached the end. This is deeply disturbing because his thinking did not reach a tidy end. His last writings contain very germinal thoughts. 'This', he said, 'is the end, for me the beginning of life.' We might almost say the same of his theology. There are few writers who have influenced the Church more during the past quarter of this century and it is not only what he has written and thought and taught which has influenced us, but the lines he started. His thinking has gone on. If we read this volume with understanding, we come to the end with a deep sense of unease. The lines he drew can be shown; but where do they lead us now? We must go on.

I. THE CHURCH

There is considerable confusion about what Bonhoeffer taught concerning the future of the Church. His earliest theses were concerned with the Church and at every point of his career he faced honestly the question of the Church's structure. His task in the 'Church Struggle' was that of insisting that the Confessing Church was a Church not a movement. He examined ruthlessly the boundaries of the Church and the whole issue of church union.[1] While he could not regard the pro-Nazi 'German Christians' as being members of the Church, he championed the cause of including Lutheran and Reformed within the same Confessing Church. He insisted upon the right of each Church to examine and teach its own historic confessions.

Anyone who has read the first two volumes in this series will have recognized Bonhoeffer as a Lutheran, with Luther's high

[1] page 71.

doctrine of the Church. When he quarrelled with Lutherans over the nature of the Church, it was always to maintain a position more Lutheran than that of his opponents. This meant that he considered the Church to have three permanent elements whatever changes there might be in its historical form. The Church exists, according to Bonhoeffer, in his most uncompromising Lutheran mood, to proclaim the gospel, to administer the sacraments, and to demonstrate the *sanctorum communio*. He never departed from this view and towards the end of his life it enabled him to look fearlessly at the reform of the Church. He was confident that the Church would survive if it maintained these three elements. At the end, he saw the need for reform – the Church should have no possessions or endowments; the clergy should live on the free-will offerings of their congregations. Much would change – but the Church, with its essential structure unimpaired, would survive.[1] These are some of the 'conclusions' he lists in the third part of his 'Outline for a Book'. The earlier parts deal with 'A Stock-taking of Christianity' and 'The Real Meaning of Christian Faith'.

If Bonhoeffer had lived he would have written that book. He said that it would be 'not more than 100 pages'. A miracle for a German theologian! Far from dismissing worship or theology as outworn, he intended to devote a great deal of space to the discovery of a 'cultus' for today and a meaningful theology for a world come of age. Certainly he would have attacked our accepted ideas of God, of the Church and of worship; but he would also have attacked our understanding of the world.

Since the publication of *Letters and Papers from Prison*, which contains his 'Outline for a Book', no study has appeared which

---

[1] page 109.

seriously considers what he wanted to say in his unwritten book. Yet, since it was to be about the Church, it is there that we must look for his ongoing ideas.[1]

The subject of the first chapter was to be Christianity and it was here he began that stocktaking with a discussion of 'the coming of age of mankind'. It is important to recognize that he considered that historically this process started in the thirteenth century with the Renaissance. To this he linked the different kind of world which the second industrial revolution had brought into being. The goal of the world we now live in is to be independent of nature. 'Nature was formerly conquered by spiritual means, with us by technical organizations of all kinds. Our immediate environment is not nature, as formerly, but organization.'

It is thus that he states the problem of the Church of today, changed as it is by the changes in the world. The process that started in the thirteenth century as an upsurge of the spirit of man, a liberation from magic, has in our century become a liberation from nature. Bonhoeffer sees this development as good, but dangerous. We do not live in a safe world. Immunity from the control of nature, which really means immunity from unknown causes, produces a new crop of dangers. Bonhoeffer notes, but does not develop the idea, that the very organization is dangerous. To be able to control nature by our technology does not imply that we have been liberated. It means that we now face the problem of living with our technology – which brings with it the need for a new 'spiritual force'.

By throwing the problem back at man Bonhoeffer has not dealt with this situation adequately in his writings. 'Man is

---

[1] *Letters and Papers from Prison*, the enlarged edition, SCM Press, London, 1971, pp. 380-3. Macmillan, N.Y., paperback ed.

again thrown back on himself' is insufficient. Had he lived, no doubt he would have developed this thesis further. He is dealing with a new kind of man, because the man 'come of age' is not the same man as the one who wrestled with nature. He is a man who has created 'the organization' in a way that man never created nature. We have no quarrel with his belief in the need for a new spiritual vitality. But what is 'spiritual' in a world come of age? Bonhoeffer saw that religion had decayed, that we could no longer simply talk of 'God' in a way that all would understand. What then would be the new spiritual vitality? The few hints which are left are important.

Bonhoeffer did not see much hope in a revival of Pietism, which he regarded as 'a last attempt to maintain evangelical Christianity as a religion'. He had little time for the attempts of unorthodox Lutheranism to rescue the Church 'as an institution for salvation'. He found more hope in the experience of the Confessing Church and its attempts to develop a theology of revelation. He never regarded this as a narrow subject, as Barth did. Theology was not narrow for Bonhoeffer.

The attempt to work out a theology of revelation which would go beyond Karl Barth led him to relate his theology to the search of art and science to find a foundation. He was not leading back to a natural theology. He was too much of a Barthian for that; but he was seeking an understanding of revelation which would provide a basis for art and science also. He wanted one world inhabited by one kind of man. He had no time for a religious man, an artistic man, a scientific man. Somewhere there must be a way to understand *man*. He believed that 'somewhere' to be the Church.

For Bonhoeffer, the Church is a part of the world. Sometimes it appears to be a particularly nasty piece of the world, but it is that part of the world where man discovers himself and it is where spiritual vitality is provided. He saw the dangers of the Church on the defensive, unwilling to take risks in the service of humanity. It is significant that no sooner has he raised this point than he notes, as the conclusion to his chapter of 'stocktaking': 'Public morals – as shown by sexual behaviour.' Bonhoeffer would be at the centre of the present debate on the permissive society, indeed much of what he has written on ethics is relevant and of permanent value on this subject, and it is significant that he cannot deal with his chapter on the stocktaking of Christianity without raising the issue of 'changes in sexual behaviour'.

When Bonhoeffer touches upon the real meaning of the Christian faith, he at once deals with 'worldliness and God'. He attempts to retain these two ideas side by side, because he will not accept abstract ideas of God's omnipotence as a genuine experience of God. He stresses that God must be experienced in the heart of our worldliness. Encounter with Jesus Christ is the key to man's understanding of God, of a transcendent life and of the spiritual. This encounter must first be seen as an orientation of the human life in the experience of Jesus as 'the man for others'. It is in this understanding of Jesus that Bonhoeffer develops his unique definition of transcendence. He is in the tradition of Kierkegaard and Barth when he attacks religion, or when he refuses to accept transcendence as a religious relationship to an absolute power. This is part of his attack on metaphysics, which, he maintains, places God outside the experience of the world, ready to come in only as a rescuer.

We did not need Bonhoeffer to attack this theory. Every 'incarnational' theologian has seen that an impassive God – 'Immortal, invisible, God only wise' – is irreconcilable with the incarnation of Jesus Christ. But Bonhoeffer pressed home the logic of this view. According to him, transcendence is understood in Jesus, not in his relationship to an absolute God, but in his concern for others. This freedom from self, maintained to the point of death, not some special relationship, is the sole ground of his omnipotence, omniscience and ubiquity.

It is in his *Christology* that Bonhoeffer explains his attitude to transcendence, which lies at the heart of all worship. We have need to pursue this line much further, as I am sure Bonhoeffer would have done had he lived. Our relation to God, which is what we all mean by worship in the Church, is not a religious relationship, but a new life for others by participation in the 'being of God'. Then transcendence becomes related to the nearest thing at hand, not to tasks beyond our powers for which we have to bring in some superhuman aid.

Bonhoeffer makes this the starting point for a reinterpretation of biblical terminology, and this is the real setting for that other phrase with which Bonhoeffer has been associated – 'religionless Christianity'. Bonhoeffer himself described this as 'the non-religious interpretation of biblical concepts'. Among these concepts he lists 'creation, fall, atonement, repentance, faith, the new life, the last things'.

But before we can talk of the implications of all this for the Church, we need to ask the basic question, 'What do we really believe?' Not, what do you have to believe to be a Christian? But, we believers, what do we really believe? This is of the same order as the question, 'What is Jesus Christ for us today?' Bonhoeffer puts the question with force – What do we believe to the extent that we are prepared to die for it? He will not accept the subterfuge that it is not *our* faith, but that of the Church. Neither will he follow the dialectical theologians with their 'We have no control over our faith'. We cannot escape giving an answer; the question must be answered by us because we are the Church. All that has been said about worldliness, about what we mean by God, about transcendence, about the man for others and a non-religious interpretation of biblical concepts comes to the flood in the honest question which each man must answer – What do we really believe? The answer to that question has overwhelming importance for our understanding of the Church.

If the life of Jesus and that of his followers is the life for others, if only in an orientation of our life are we able to know transcendence, then the Church too is being its true self when it exists for others.

It was in drawing this conclusion that Bonhoeffer, looking at his own Lutheran Church, insisted that the logic of such consequences was that the Church should give away all its privileges. It does not exist for itself or in itself. The Church exists for humanity; it must tell men, whatever their calling, what it means to live in Christ, to exist for others. When Bonhoeffer points out that the Church must pay more attention to 'human example', he is not simply saying that the Church must devote itself to good works rather than to theology. He retained that high regard which all Germans have for theology. Rather he is pointing to a neglected aspect of New Testament study, the importance of human example, which he sees as having its origin in Jesus and as rated highly by Paul. The references to Jesus and Paul refer to the way in which they communicated as well as to the quality of their lives. He expressly states that he hopes 'to take up later this subject of "example" and its place in the New Testament' and comments that 'it is something that we have almost entirely forgotten'. Bonhoeffer admits that what he has written in prison must sound 'crude and condensed'. He wanted, but did not have time, 'to say simply and clearly – things that we so often like to shirk'. Our best service to Bonhoeffer is to go on and do the things he planned.

2. ETHICS

Eberhard Bethge has produced the book *Ethics*[1] by Dietrich Bonhoeffer, which contains the texts he had written on this subject up to the time when he was arrested on 5th April, 1943. He never completed the book, but the subject recurs so often in his later letters that we can do a great deal to clarify what is contained in the published fragments. *Ethics* as it stands is not the book Dietrich Bonhoeffer intended to publish. It is a compilation of what has been preserved. The order is not his, and for this reason we may miss the systematic thought which is so typical of Bonhoeffer's work. However, there is enough material in this book to show the direction in which he was travelling.

Two important quotes remind us of the place he gave to his work on *Ethics*. First, in a letter addressed to Eberhard Bethge, dated 18th November, 1943: 'I've reproached myself for not having finished my *Ethics* . . . and it was some consolation to me that I had told you the essentials, and that even if you had forgotten it, it would probably emerge again indirectly somehow. Besides, my ideas were still incomplete.'[2] Then four weeks later: 'I sometimes feel as if my life were more or less over, and as if all I had to do now were to finish my *Ethics*.'[3]

Over the next sixteen months, all spent in prison, he tested out many of the things that he wrote in the unfinished text and he added comments in letters to Bethge and attempted to put new insights, however tentative, into poems and those frag-

---

[1] SCM Press, London, 1955. Macmillan, N.Y., paperback ed.   [2] *Letters and Papers from Prison*, p. 129.   [3] Ibid., p. 163.

ments of a novel and a drama which are introduced in this third volume.

The unfinished text of *Ethics*, some comments preserved by Bethge, a few letters, these fragments are all that Bonhoeffer wrote on this subject. Yet these are sufficient to establish that he pointed a way which led to 'situational ethics', and also that much of what has been written on the subject, particularly in America, is a divergence rather than a development of Bonhoeffer's thought. Too often situational ethics has rejected not only ethical systems which Bonhoeffer too put on one side, but also ethical guidelines and insights upon which he depended. There are indications in this third volume of his papers that he had already seen the way in which we might go forward.

Had he lived, I suspect that Bonhoeffer would have found the writings of Teilhard de Chardin encouraging and exciting. No one can pretend that the two men are similar. When I tried to write an imaginary dialogue between him and Teilhard for the Third Programme of the BBC, I had the utmost difficulty in finding a common point on which to introduce the conversation. But once found, the writing flowed. If these two had met, they would have discussed how to arrive at an ethical decision.

But let us look at the point which Bonhoeffer reached in his *Ethics*. He saw that the lack of interest in ethical systems arose, not from ethical indifference, on the contrary, 'it arises from the fact that our period . . . is oppressed by a superabounding reality of concrete ethical problems'.[1] There can be little doubt that we are still in the same period. Systems may be rejected, but the 'permissive' society is wrongly named. It is rather the 'ethically neurotic' society. A rejection of older systems means an overwhelming need to take ethical decisions

---

[1] *Ethics*, p. 3.

without the help of any rules. Not only systems, but attitudes also have proved inadequate. Bonhoeffer's list in *Ethics*, of those attitudes with which we are no longer able to face the ethical problems of our day, is terribly relevant because the years have emphasized how inadequate they are – the reasonable man, the fanatic, the man with a conscience, the path of duty, absolute freedom, private virtue. He does not pour scorn on these attitudes, which he compares to the unreality of the weapons of Don Quixote, but they fail.[1]

This passage at the beginning of *Ethics* gave the title to the first of my three volumes of Bonhoeffer's papers – *No Rusty Swords*. He saw that to trust in the old attitudes was as useless as to use old systems of ethics. Such inadequacy was like an old world venturing to take up arms against a new one, as 'when a world of the past hazards an attack against the superior forces of the commonplace and the mean'. The honourable attitudes of the past he compared to *rusty swords*. Then came his formula, which has still not been fully developed – 'A man can hold his own here only if he can combine *simplicity* with *wisdom*.'[2] Bonhoeffer did not himself explain all that he meant by simplicity or wisdom, but he gave many examples of both. His most attractive example of simplicity is in his insistence that man does not make moral decisions all the time! 'In historical human existence', he writes, 'everything has its time – eating, drinking and sleeping, as well as deliberate resolve and action, rest as well as work, purposelessness as well as the fulfilment of purpose, inclination as well as duty, play as well as earnest endeavour, joy as well as renunciation.'[3]

It is not only in his *Ethics* that Bonhoeffer insists upon life being more than a series of moral decisions. He sees that moral decisions can only be made clearly if they are made as part of

---

[1] Ibid., p. 6.   [2] Ibid., p. 7.
[3] Ibid., pp. 232–3.

a fuller life in which most of the time one is not thinking about moral decisions. Within the limits of a full life a man must find time to discuss what is right and what is wrong, but if this becomes an obsession with him so that he thinks of nothing else, then he is in danger of a pathological overburdening of life by the ethical.

In the complex arguments he used at his trial, Bonhoeffer did not stop every time he tried a subterfuge to consider whether he was right or wrong to lie. He was not overburdened by a set of rules or by a constant consideration of the ethical. And here he seems to be developing an attitude to ethics which is of special importance in our complex world. He does not in fact say that there are no guidelines. His careful treatment of 'Suicide' in his *Ethics*[1] shows that he has clear ideas of what he means by the dignity and responsibility of man. 'Man, unlike the beasts, does not carry his life as a compulsion which he cannot throw off.'[2] He recognizes both freedom and responsibility. The latter he understands in the sense of Richard Niebuhr's *'responsibility* as the response to a situation'. The wrongfulness of suicide, for example, is to be 'arraigned not before the forum of morality or of men but solely before the forum of God'.[3] It would appear that what he is doing here is cutting a path through the ethical jungle of our time, a path which is neither limited by the traditions of the elders nor wasted in the unmarked territory of so-called situational ethics. These have undoubtedly developed largely since his time. Bonhoeffer comes near to situational ethics only because he sees the inadequacy of the old weapons.

He admirably combined his simplicity and wisdom in his whole attitude to the Resistance. He was prepared to be a conspirator, though not always a very clever one! He threw

[1] Ibid., pp. 122-8. [2] Ibid., p. 122. [3] Ibid., p. 123.

himself into the plans for 'Operation 7',[1] and eventually also for the elimination of Hitler. There is no indication that he was making heavy weather of defending his actions. He came out into the tempest of living with the zest of a man who loved life and action. But he was not thoughtless. All his theological acumen was used when necessary. However, it was not used all the time. When he discussed conspiracy he did not treat his fellow-conspirators to a theological discussion, nor compel them to examine all their ethical assumptions. He saw what had to be done and did it. He was healthy and full of zest in the way in which he tackled the job at hand. Yet when he felt uncertainty he looked wisely into the situation and applied theological tests of great severity and honesty.

There is a good example given by Dr Bell, the late Bishop of Chichester, in his account of the meetings in Sweden.[2] Schönfeld had outlined the plan for eliminating Hitler and taking over the government. It seemed simple and convincing. Even the Russians would understand. Bell was convinced, but Bonhoeffer, he says, 'was obviously distressed in his mind as to the lengths to which he had been driven by force of circumstances in the plot for the elimination of Hitler. The Christian conscience, he said, was not quite at ease with Schönfeld's ideas.' Then Bell quotes Bonhoeffer, and just as we are expecting him to say that a Christian can hardly be happy about assassination, he surprises us by showing his concern over a solution which looks as though it might be too easy! Here are his words as Bell quotes them: 'There must be punishment by God. We should not be worthy of such a solution. We do not want to escape repentance. Our action must be understood as an act of repentance.'

Bonhoeffer has done two basic things in the field of ethics.

[1] page 131.   [2] pages 170ff.

First, he has rejected the concept of 'formation', which means imposing a Christian point of view on society, and replaced it by 'conformation',[1] which means being conformed to the life of Christ – 'the man for others', 'sharing in the sufferings of God', etc. A careful reading of this third volume will lead us to see that Bonhoeffer had already entered into the problems emerging in Germany at the end of the war and familiar to us today. We do not have so many guides in this emotional jungle that we can afford to ignore the wise counsel of one who lived between the principles of wisdom and simplicity, who would never refuse to face the issue by trusting in a set of rules or declaring the issue none of his concern. As a Christian pastor, Bonhoeffer accepted the burden of pastoral concern, but did not determine beforehand how each ethical decision should be taken. A casuistic solution to the world's ethical problems was no longer possible, and a 'situational' solution which left the individual without guidance or comfort was like the 'cheap grace' which he had early rejected in *The Cost of Discipleship*.

By selecting two major themes in Bonhoeffer's writings, both amply illustrated in the three volumes of which this is the last, I have tried to show that the value of these letters and papers lies, not so much in the answers they give to our contemporary problems as in the insights they provide for us in the daily questioning and constant ethical decisions we all have to face. Bonhoeffer provides us with a personal example and a body of careful thinking which can help a man to cope in this world.

In this introduction I have chosen two themes. There are many others. They include a total rethinking of our attitude as Christians to the use of violence, either by forces of law and order or by the rebels, a reassessment of the relationship of

---

[1] *Ethics*, pp. 17ff.

Church and State, Christology, our understanding of man, sacred and secular, and so forth. Bonhoeffer gives few answers to our questions, but he sets us thinking in an effective way, which demands courage and honesty, initiative and action, the life of man in all its activity, and the preparation for a fuller life, into which he has now entered.

E. H. ROBERTSON

Westbourne Park, 1973

PART ONE

The Theologian in Wartime

1939 *September* – First conspiracy talks between Josef Müller, Dohnanyi and Oster.

October – Conspirators with Beck seek contact with England through the Vatican.

November – Memorandum by Dohnanyi, Oster and Gisevius delivered to the Chief of Staff, General Halder. Failure of attempt to overthrow Hitler.

1940 *1st February* – Completion of 'peace' document for England by Josef Müller and Dohnanyi, for delivery to Beck and Halder.

18th March – Closing of Sigurdshof by Gestapo.

11th June – Italy enters the war beside Germany.

17th June – French capitulation.

22nd June – Armistice at Compiègne.

14th July – Dissolution of study conference in Blöstau.

August – Bonhoeffer talks with Oster and Dohnanyi about extra-parochial duties and work for the *Abwehr*.

4th September – Bonhoeffer forbidden to speak in public and required to report regularly to the police.

September–October – Work on *Ethics* at Klein-Krössin.

30th October – Appointed to the *Abwehr* office at Munich.

17th November – Visit to Benedictine monastery at Ettal.

1941 *24th February–24th March* – First wartime journey to Switzerland.

27th March – Bonhoeffer forbidden to print or publish.

6th May – Twenty-three leaders of the Confessing Church arrested.

22nd June – Invasion of Russia.

29th August–26th September – Second visit to Switzerland. – Comments with Visser 't Hooft on Paton's book, *The Church and the New Order*.

1. Absorbed in Theology

When Bonhoeffer returned to Germany after his brief stay in America, hardly anyone understood the great decision he had taken. The war clouds were gathering and Bonhoeffer's personal struggles mattered to few. He returned to take up his duties as before with the collective pastorates of Köslin and Sigurdshof. Groups of his ordinands spent a Baltic holiday with him, but this was interrupted by the news that war was imminent. He returned to his parents' home in Berlin. With the outbreak of war there was confusion. Niemöller was in prison and there were fears for his life. Yet news broke that he had volunteered for war service. War brought casualties to the ordinands who had been called up and Bonhoeffer began a series of circular letters which kept him in touch with his students during the separation of war service. His first circular letter of the war was reproduced in The Way to Freedom *(pp. 250–5). A letter from the Bishop of Chichester assured him of understanding during the dark days ahead:*

6th September, 1939

CHICHESTER TO BONHOEFFER: You know how deeply I feel for you and yours in this melancholy time. May God comfort and guide you. I think often of our talk in the summer. May He keep you. Let us pray together often by reading the Beatitudes; *Pax Dei quae superat omnia nos custodiat.*

When the campaign in Poland was over the leaders of the Old Prussian Council of Brethren decided to continue the collectiv pastorates in Köslin and Sigurdshof. There were still ordinands who needed further training and the war proved less disturbing to the work than had been expected. Köslin was closed that autumn, but Sigurdshof lasted on into 1940. Bonhoeffer gave his undivided attention to theology. He made some progress with his commentary on Psalm 119 and began a series of theological letters. These were circulated to his former students and to others in the Confessing Church. One he sent for Christmas shows the development of his thought especially in the field of Christology at that period:

Christmas 1939

BONHOEFFER TO THE BRETHREN: No priest, no theologian stood at the cradle in Bethlehem. And yet all Christian theology has its origin in the wonder of all wonders, that God became man. 'Alongside the brilliance of the holy night there burns the fire of the unfathomable mystery of theology.' *Theologia sacra* arises from those on bended knees who do homage to the mystery of the divine child in the stall. Israel had no theology. She did not know God in the flesh. Without the holy night there is no theology. 'God revealed in the flesh', the God-man Jesus Christ, is the holy mystery which theology is appointed to guard. What a mistake to think that it is the task of theology to unravel God's mystery, to bring it down to the flat, ordinary human wisdom of experience and reason! It is the task of theology solely to preserve God's wonder as wonder, to understand, to defend, to glorify God's mystery as mystery. This and nothing else was the intention of the ancient Church when it fought with unflagging zeal over the mystery of the persons of the Trinity and the natures of Jesus Christ. How superficial and flippant, especially of theologians, to send theology to the knacker's yard, to make out that one is not a theologian and doesn't want to be, and in so doing to ridicule one's own ministry and ordination and in the end to have, and to advocate, a bad theology instead of a good one! But of course, where in our theological classes were we shown and taught the mystery of God in the flesh, the birth of Jesus Christ, the God-man and saviour, as the unfathomable mystery of God? Where do we hear it preached? Surely Christmas Eve can kindle in us again something like a love of sacred theology, so that, seized and compelled by the wonder of the cradle of the Son of God, we are moved to consider again, reverently, the mysteries of God. But it may well be that the glow of the divine mysteries has already been quenched, and has died in our hearts as well.

The ancient Church meditated on the question of Christ for several centuries. It imprisoned reason in obedience to Jesus Christ, and in harsh, conflicting sentences gave living witness to the mystery of the person of Jesus Christ. It did not give way to the modern pretence that this mystery could only be felt or experienced, for it knew the corruption and self-deception of all human feeling and experience. Nor, of course, did it think that this mystery could be thought out logically, but by being unafraid to express the ultimate conceptual paradoxes, it bore witness to, and glorified, the mystery as a mystery against all reason. The Christology of the ancient Church really arose at the cradle of Bethlehem, and the brightness of Christmas lies on its weather-beaten face. Even today, it wins the hearts of all who come to know it. So at Christmas time we should again go to school with the ancient Church and seek to understand in worship what it thought and taught, to glorify and to defend belief in Christ. The hard concepts of that time are like stones from which one strikes fire.

Let us look briefly at three well-known christological principles, which survive in our Lutheran confessions, not only that we might preach them to the congregations, but to put our thought and knowledge, as preachers of the word, to work in the light of the holy night.

1. The Fathers were concerned to say that God, the Son,

took upon himself *human nature*, not that he took upon himself *a man*. What does that mean? God became man by taking upon himself human nature, not by taking an individual man. This distinction was necessary to preserve the universality of the wonder of Christmas. 'Human nature', that is, the nature, essence, flesh of all men, i.e. my nature, my flesh; human nature, that is, the embodiment of all human possibilities. Perhaps we moderns might put it more simply by saying that in the birth of Jesus Christ, God took manhood, and not just an individual man. But this taking happened corporeally, and that is the unique wonder of the incarnation. The body of Jesus Christ is our flesh. He bears our flesh. Therefore, where Jesus Christ is, there we are, whether we know it or not; that is true because of the incarnation. What happens to Jesus Christ, happens to us. It really is all *our* 'poor flesh and blood' which lies there in the crib; it is *our* flesh which dies with him on the cross and is buried with him. He took human nature so that we might be eternally with him. Where the body of Jesus Christ is, there are we; indeed, we are his body. So the Christmas message for all men runs: You are accepted, God has not despised you, but he bears in his body all your flesh and blood. Look at the cradle! In the body of the little child, in the incarnate son of God, your flesh, all your distress, anxiety, temptation, indeed all your sin, is borne, forgiven and healed. If you complain, 'My nature, My whole being is beyond salvation and I must be eternally lost', the Christmas message replies, 'Your nature, your whole being is accepted; Jesus bears it, in this way he has become your saviour.' Because Christmas is the physical acceptance of all human flesh by the gracious God, we must affirm that God's son took human nature upon himself.

2. 'Two natures and one person' – the ancient Church has ventured to express its knowledge of Christmas in this

olstice long before Christmas was celebrated. Its origins are obscure. It is certain that for a long time four different events were commemorated on this day: the birth of Christ, the baptism of Christ, the marriage at Cana and the arrival of the Magi from the East. In his article on 'The Origins of the Feast of the Epiphany' (*Gesammelte Aufsätze* II, pp. 123 ff.), Karl Holl has attempted to derive the peculiar structure of the festival from the Egyptian Aeon feast which was celebrated on the night of the 5th–6th January and coincided with the drawing of water from the Nile and a miracle of wine. However that may be, since the fourth century, the Church has solemnly celebrated the birth of Christ on 25th December and has detached it from the feast of the Epiphany. Furthermore, Rome transferred the consecration of water, which was connected with baptism, to the day before Easter; the marriage at Cana was moved to the later festival period, so that only the worship of Christ by the wise men from the East, the 'appearing of the star before the Gentiles', came to occupy the central place in the Epiphany. Nevertheless, the liturgies of the Western Churches show that even here the original content of the feast was not wholly lost. So a certain indefiniteness about Epiphany remained. In view of the historical evidence, it is a dogmatic and pedagogic simplification for us to say today that Epiphany is the feast of the manifestation of the Godhead of Jesus Christ before the world. But in practice the content of the feast can be reduced to this or a similar formula.

The detachment of the feast of the birth of Christ from the day of his baptism was of great significance. In gnostic and heretical circles in the East the idea had developed that it was the day of Christ's baptism which was really the day of his birth as Son of God. In addition, an artificial reckoning had been made, according to which Jesus was thirty years old on the day of his baptism. That gives us cause to consider for a

paradoxical dogmatic formula. 'Ventured', for it, too, knew that something inexpressible was expressed here, simply because one could not be silent about it (Augustine). People found two things in the cradle, and bore witness to them: manhood taken in the flesh and the eternal Godhead, both united in the one name Jesus Christ, human and divine nature united in the person of the Son of God. Divine nature, that is, the Godhead: the Father, Son and Holy Spirit united for ever. It is the eternal might, glory and majesty of the triune God. Wherever the Son is, he brings this divine nature with him, for he remains true God from eternity to eternity. If the Son of God has truly become man, the divine nature is certainly also present in all its majesty; otherwise Christ would not be true God. This really is so: if Jesus Christ is not true God, how could he *help* us? If Christ is not true man, how could he help *us*? Of course, the divine nature is hidden in the cradle, and it shines through the poor rags of the human nature only here and there in the life of Jesus. But however mysteriously hidden, it is still present, hidden for us, present for us. Divine and human nature, united in Christ and still not made one; for otherwise the vast difference between Godhead and manhood would be done away with. So it may never be said that the divine nature assumed the human nature; that would imply that the Father and the Holy Ghost also took flesh, and would thus mean the ultimate (modalistic, idealistic, pantheistic, Schleiermacherian) confusion of God and man. No, it means that the Son of God, the divine person of the Logos, took human nature. But Godhead and manhood, divine nature and human nature, met and united only in the *person* of the Son of God, in Jesus Christ. Nowhere else but in and through the person of Jesus Christ are Godhead and manhood united, 'without confusion, without change, without division, without separation', as the Chalcedonian definition put it in a supreme paradox, and at the same time in a most reverent preservation of the mystery of the person of the Mediator. Rarely in later ages has reason been so ready to humble and surrender itself before the miracle of God as it does in these words. But precisely because of that, reason has been made a better instrument for the glorification of the divine revelation. The christological formula, 'Two natures, one person', at the same time has supreme soteriological significance: Godhead and manhood separated from one another before Christ came, united with each other only in the incarnation of the Son of God. Only through the person do the natures have communion with each other, i.e. only through Jesus Christ are Godhead and manhood united.

3. The contribution of the Lutheran Church, added to the ancient Church's Christology, consisted in the doctrine of the *genus majestaticum* (disputed most vigorously by Reformed theologians), i.e. the doctrine of the mediation of the properties of the divine nature to the human nature which took place in the incarnation. 'For to make alive, to have all judgement and power in heaven and on earth, to have all things in his hands, to have subjected all things under his feet, to purify from sin, etc., are not created gifts, but divine, infinite properties, which according to the testimony of Scripture are still given and supplied to the *man* Christ' (Formula of Concord, S.D. VII 55). True, it remains incomprehensible how the human nature, which is our nature, should share the properties of the divine majesty, but this is scriptural doctrine, and it expresses the deepest and ultimate union of God with man thus, so that one can now say with Luther: 'Wherever you can say "Here is God", you must also say, "So Christ the man is also there". And if you could point to a place where there was God and not man, the person would already be divided. No, friend, where you show me God you must also show me man.' 'It is

the glory of our Lord God that he condescends flesh.' Lutheran teaching parried the objection Church that the human nature was no longer by referring to the unique miracle, and to So only from this standpoint do we have the righ of the Holy Eucharist and the words of the Lo body'. If Christ speaks in this way, then he mu than any man what his body is and may be. So eucharist are extremely closely connected. The *genus majestaticum* illuminates this connection. who came in the flesh for our salvation gives with his body and blood in the sacrament. 'The of God is bodiliness' (Oetinger).

The thoughts that we have expressed here ar they are minute fragments of the edifice of Christology. But it is not a question of our ma building, but of our being led by one thought read and to consider more reverently and more biblical witness of the mystery of the incarnatio perhaps also to sing Luther's Christmas hymns fully and more joyfully.

G.

And one month later he was developing similar thoug young ordinands preach more meaningfully, during season. He was binding them closely to the Chri strengthening their Lutheran theology! Here is meditation for Epiphany:

BONHOEFFER TO THE BRETHREN: The strange in which the feast of the Epiphany is involved is the feast itself. It is clear that Epiphany was reg Churches of East and West as the supreme feast o

moment the relationship between the birth and the baptism of Jesus Christ. It was usual in the ancient Church, and Augustine testifies to this, to celebrate the day of one's rebirth, of baptism, rather than one's proper birthday. Now it seemed natural to do the same with the day of Jesus' baptism and to make this the main festival. But this brought with it the possibility of a dangerous error, namely, a neglect of the incarnation of God. The birth of Jesus is not in fact the natural beginning of a human life, which had to be followed later by spiritual rebirth; the birth of Jesus is the incarnation of the Son of God for the salvation of all flesh. We have already seen in our reflections about Christmas that it pleased God to take human flesh, human nature, and not to 'adopt' the man Jesus as son, as the heretics taught in conflict with the ancient Church. Had God only accepted the man Jesus in baptism as his son, we would remain unredeemed; in that case, Jesus would indeed be the unattainable, solitary one, the superman, who attained salvation for himself, but he would not be able to help the rest of us. But if Jesus is the Son of God, who has taken our own flesh and blood right from his birth, even his conception, then he alone is true man and true God; he alone can help us. But in that case, 'the saving hour has struck' indeed for us at his birth; in that case the birth of Christ is the salvation of all men, and the incarnation of the Son of God is the day which makes our rebirth possible. Christ's birth and our rebirth belong together, but not Christ's baptism and our baptism. That sheds light on the significance of Jesus' baptism. If it is not the day of the adoption of the Son of God, then what is it? If Jesus desires baptism, then he does so, unlike all other men, as the one who alone is good, sinless, in no need of forgiveness. But as the one who is good he desires baptism, not for himself, but for the sake of those who need it, for sinners. Precisely as the one who alone is good, he does not allow himself to be distinguished from sinners, he does not become a Pharisee, who wants to separate the good for himself. The sinlessness, the goodness of Jesus shows itself precisely in his unconditional love of sinners. Jesus goes to be baptized, not in repentance, but in love, and in so doing he stands on the side of sinners. John tries to refuse him baptism because he does not understand what Jesus is doing. The baptism is Jesus' self-humiliation for the sake of sinners. He, the sinless, becomes a sinner for the sake of his brethren. Nowhere in the whole of Scripture is there an indication that Jesus needed baptism for his own sake; indeed, all the evidence emphatically points in the opposite direction. Jesus desires baptism solely as the one whose goodness consists in his fellowship with sinners; so he undergoes baptism, 'for thus it is fitting for us to fulfil all righteousness' (Matt. 3. 15). This 'all' righteousness, however, is not a self-seeking holiness, but the perfect love of God for men, for sinners. This moment is the fellowship of the Son of God with sinners in baptism, in which it is confirmed to him (and to the bystanders, cf. John 1. 31 f., Matt. 3. 17, and textual variants) by his heavenly Father that he *is* his dear son. As the saviour of sinners, Jesus is proclaimed as the one he was from the beginning, i.e. the Son of God. The baptism is a confirmation of what Jesus is on the Godward side. It does not add anything new to his being, but it brings something decisively new in his action; for from now on Jesus acts before all the world as the one he is from eternity. The manifestation of Jesus as Son of God, as it is celebrated at Epiphany in commemoration of Jesus' baptism, is an appearance in lowliness, in equality with sinners. The companion of tax collectors and sinners is the Son of God, whose appearance we should welcome.

It is just the same in the case of the other two aspects of the feast of the Epiphany, the appearance of the star to the wise men and the marriage at Cana. The star was not a sign which visibly announced the birth of the king of the Jews to all the world. It had to be recognized and believed. Herod did not see it. It rose among the Gentiles and summoned them to Jerusalem. So Epiphany is in a particular way the feast of Gentile Christendom, 'our feast'. But the Gentile wise men would not have found the way without the testimony of Holy Scripture. The wonderful summons of the star is followed by the summons to believe in the promise of God in Scripture. Otherwise the wise men would not have known and honoured the child of Bethlehem as king. The manifestation of the divinity of Jesus Christ consists here simply in a summons to believe in the poor child in the cradle.

The wedding feast at Cana reports the 'first sign that Jesus did' to manifest his glory, an extremely miraculous and, to our minds, almost an unnecessary sign of his divine glory, in view of the triviality of the occasion. But the decisive thing is that this sign of the divine power of Jesus remains hidden from the guests, the toastmaster, the bridegroom; it merely serves the faith of the disciples. Jesus will not compel recognition of himself as Son of God through magic and wonders, but he calls for faith in his divine status. 'His disciples believed in him.' The glory of Jesus is hidden in his lowliness, and is seen only in faith. Here, the content of the feast of the Epiphany is closely connected with the Christmas story, so we can understand how the day of the Epiphany was at the same time the manifestation of the one who 'had no form or comeliness' (Isa. 53. 2). So Epiphany points to the time which now follows in the Church's year, to the Passion. It makes good sense that the last pericope of the Epiphany season should be the transfiguration of Jesus, on the way to Jerusalem.

G.S.III pp. 388–92

*These theological letters were added as supplements to the circular
letters which he sent every month to the Brethren of the Pomeranian
Confessing Church. The supplement to his February 1940 letter
raised controversy. It was on the subject of the Lord's Supper.
Eberhard Baumann of the Reformed Church raised serious objections
and the theological commission of the Pomeranian Council of
Brethren was brought to life by this controversy. Bonhoeffer had a
way of making theologians rethink their theology. Here is the text
of the offending supplement:*

ON THE LAST SUPPER

*An introduction to the study of article VII of the Lutheran
Formula of Concord*

We are approaching the period of well-attended, frequent and
elaborate celebrations of the Lord's Supper, of the final confirmation classes, in which many thousands of young Christians
are being prepared for their first approach to the sacrament.
This and Passiontide itself will always be the occasion for the
minister to reflect on the last gift of Jesus to his disciples. To
meditate on the Last Supper – but should we really do that?
Have not attempts to explain the Last Supper been for a
thousand years the cause of more division than clarity in the
Church? Has not the meal of reconciliation and brotherly love
not become in theory virtually a sign of division and dispute?
In the end, has not everything that can possibly be said on this
question already been said in the course of the centuries?
Would it not be better simply to practise and to receive the
sacrament and to refrain from all thought about it? It is
certainly true that more harm is done through a deficiency in
the practice, both of repentance and of the Lord's Supper,
than by inadequate preaching on the meaning of the Last
Supper! Right thoughts only come from right practice. But

what is the right practice of the Last Supper? What may we expect from receiving the sacrament? What is the gift in which we share? What did Jesus promise in instituting the Last Supper, and what is the right preaching as people are invited to the Lord's Table?

We cannot avoid the fact that the Last Supper is not an obscure mystical experience but is concerned with the clear, incarnate word of God, the promise and demand of Jesus Christ. Jesus himself did not give the disciples bread and wine in silence, but he spoke his word over them. By celebrating this sacrament with such emphasis and such solemnity, the Lutheran Church has been concerned to continue to pronounce this word of Jesus (which still, like all preaching, cannot simply be repetition and declamation of the word of the Bible); in other words, it has been concerned that nothing else should happen in the Church other than the words and actions of Jesus himself. Nothing is to happen in the Church or to be authoritative for it other than Jesus' word and action. Because the Lutheran Church saw the introduction of human thinking into the Last Supper, both by the Roman and the Reformed doctrines of the Eucharist, it challenged the smallest details in the name of Jesus Christ. The Lutheran Church entered this struggle, not to express profound thoughts of its own about the Eucharist, but, on the contrary, to avoid all arbitrary human thoughts and to allow only the word and action of Jesus to apply and to stand in its original purity. All theological thought here stood at the service of the true and unfalsified use of the sacrament in the Church. Only where the Church – despite all the ridicule and hostility of a modern world – rests on the pure word of God and the sacraments instituted by Christ himself, can it receive the promise that the gates of hell will not prevail against it.

There is such a thing as dogmatic Pharisaism, but there is

just as frequently – and still more frequently today – an anti-dogmatic Pharisaism, an intellectual justification by works which cannot stand before God. The Lutheran Church has made its way between the two extremes in its doctrine of the Eucharist, guided solely by the word of God. It has thought, where thought was necessary, and it has kept thought within its limits. It has been able to do this by letting the sole aim of its thinking be that the miracle and the mystery of the Last Supper of Jesus Christ should be seen as such in worship.

1. The chief starting point is in the words of Christ: 'This is my body.' There is no equivocation here. The bread which we eat in the sacrament is the body of Jesus Christ. It is so by virtue of the omnipotent word of Jesus, not simply by virtue of our faith (against the *respectu fidei* of the Reformed Church). The word alone makes the sacrament, not faith. Whether it is acceptable to our reason or not, whether the world rebels or not, is of no account before the word of Jesus, which needs no confirmation from us. Either Jesus' word is valid of itself and for ever, or it is an empty shell.

2. Because the word of Jesus is true in its own strength, it also holds whether we receive the sacrament in faith or not. The bread is the body of Christ even for those who eat it unbelievingly. That is the Lutheran doctrine of the *manducatio impiorum*, which the Reformed Churches opposed. It expresses the fact that the sacrament is grounded, and stands, only in the word of Christ. Judas too received the body of Christ, of course to his own damnation. Anyone who eats unworthily 'eats judgement to himself'.

3. If Christ's word stands, then we receive the body of Christ not only spiritually, but 'orally'. Where that is denied, Christ's word is no longer taken seriously. Christ humbles himself so much, and his fellowship with us is so inward, he shows himself to each one of us so directly, that we receive his

body with our mouth and drink his blood. That is the Lutheran doctrine of the *manducatio oralis*, which was disputed by the Reformed Churches. The Lutheran Church simply sets out to take Christ at his word and to let him do his work, despite all the pride of human reason.

4. The body of Jesus Christ is 'in, with and under' the bread, 'truly and essentially present' in the sacrament. The bread does not change itself into the body (transubstantiation) – that would be human interpretation and distortion of the miracle of omnipotence, which is based solely on the word of Christ: the bread *is* the body. The word of Christ says so and makes it so.

5. The body of Christ is eaten orally and spiritually (*oraliter et spiritualiter*) in the bread. Not just orally (against Rome) – in that case the body of Jesus Christ would have become a 'thing'; but also not just spiritually (against the Reformed Church) – in that case faith, and not the word of Christ alone, would make the sacrament.

6. The union of bread and body cannot be comprehended in human terms. It may not be magically materialized (Rome) or spiritualized (the Reformed Church); in both cases the sacrament would come under man's domination. The union is something unique, incomparable, and is therefore described as 'sacramental eating'. Here, the limits of human thought, which only serves to defend the word of Jesus in its purity, are attained, and are demonstrated in the concepts of the *unio sacramentalis* and 'sacramental eating', which cannot be analysed further, but express the indissoluble wonder itself. It is not a matter of eucharistic doctrine, but of the Last Supper of Jesus Christ himself.

7. Just as the Logos entered the flesh, so the whole Christ is present in bread and wine. It is his honour in this way to enter into human nature deeply and fully, out of love towards

sinners (against the *extra-Calvinisticum*). It is Christ's will to dwell among us corporeally. Only in the body is he our saviour. So not only the 'power, influence and merits of Christ', but Christ himself physically, i.e. in his human nature, is present in the Eucharist. In Marburg, in 1529, Luther answered Oecolampadius' challenge not to hang on to the manhood of Christ but to raise himself to his Godhead, by saying that he knew and honoured no other God than the incarnate one, who is also present in the sacrament and alone can save. In the struggle of the Lutheran Church against any spiritualism, the question at stake is that of the true presence of the incarnate Son of God in his community, of Christ in the flesh.

8. 'If we do not hold to Christ's foundation, as he ordained, it is no sacrament.' Only where the 'whole action of the Last Supper' is observed in accordance with Christ's command to 'do this', where 'in a Christian assembly they take bread and wine, bless, divide, receive, eat, drink and proclaim the Lord's death', only there is the sacrament of Jesus Christ. Thus the Lutheran Church guards against all inquisitive questions about the time and duration of the sacramental union. It ties everything strictly to the command and institution, to the word, of Christ; only in the 'practice' (*usus*) or the 'action' (*actio*) is there the sacrament. Thus all questions and thoughts are strictly directed to the liturgical use of the sacrament and are limited by it. So to reflect on the Holy Communion and to protect it from misuse, superstition, secularization, curiosity, is not only permissible, but necessary, if the Last Supper is to be celebrated rightly and thankfully. So right thought comes from right usage and in its turn leads on to right usage of the sacrament.

All that has been said is summed up by Luther in the Shorter Catechism: 'What is the sacrament of the altar? It is the true body and blood of our Lord Jesus Christ to be eaten and drunk

under the bread and wine by us Christians, and appointed by
Christ himself.'   G.S.III pp. 393–8

*Considering the role which the Reformed Church had played in the
Confessing Church since Barmen in 1934 and the fact that the Old
Prussian Union of 1817 had been of Lutheran and Reformed, this
attack on the Reformed attitude to the Last Supper was bound to
raise a storm. It did. Eberhard Baumann wrote from Stettin on 12th
March, 1940, to Superintendent Onnasch of Köslin, protesting against
this so-called 'greeting' to the Confessing Church. He protested in
the name of the members who belonged to the Reformed Church and
expressed his concern about the future of the Protestant Church in
Germany if this kind of controversy was going to be encouraged in
the name of 'brotherly greeting'. He described it rather as an ex-
communication of the Reformed members. Bonhoeffer responded as
soon as he received a copy of the letter, explaining his purpose and
clearing up the misunderstanding:*

Berlin, 21st March, 1940
BONHOEFFER TO BAUMANN: Your letter to Brother Onnasch
has been sent on to me so that I might explain to you what I
meant. I am shattered by the misunderstanding of my theological letter. This letter was not intended to be a personal
interpretation of the Last Supper, nor a general exegesis, nor a
systematic piece of work. It was simply an attempt to offer
some thoughts on the seventh article of the Concordia Confession. This article has occupied my mind for a long time and
the more I work at it the more I wonder at it and love it.
These notes of mine, as is clearly marked in the copies sent,
were simply helps to pastors in their own study of the article.
I cannot think that you would fear for the future of the
Church, because such close study is being made of this particular dogmatic statement. Surely it is good that the precise sense

of the Confessions within the Confessing Church should be understood. I may add that I personally differ on several points from the Concordia Confession, as I do from the basic exegesis of Calvin's *Institutes*. But this is not my task in this letter. I do not give my own personal views or dogmatic assumptions. My task is to provide a piece of work in dogmatics for those within the Confessing Church, that they may continue to work on our Confessions. It would be a complete misunderstanding to look upon this work as a key to the future of the Confessing Church. I would say the same about commentaries on, or interpretations of, confessional statements from the Reformed Church. I have undertaken to direct ecclesiastical studies and do not consider it to be sound to neglect these dogmatic statements made by our forefathers from which we still have much to learn. Only a fundamental knowledge of the Confessions themselves can serve us as a challenge for the future.

When you say that Confessionalism is 'of the Devil' and apply this to my theological letter, I begin to wonder whether all our historical documents are to be discounted. I would welcome a study of the doctrine of the Last Supper by a brother of the Reformed Church, based upon the *Institutes*.

Be assured of my best wishes for you, my dear Konsistorialrat, that you may be richly blessed this Eastertide.

G.S.III pp. 400–1

These writings had been circulated by Superintendent Onnasch of Köslin, and without indicating any kind of authority for them or even approval, he sent a covering note saying simply: 'We are sending the enclosed article to the brethren as a greeting for Passiontide and as a suggestion for theological work.' That is why the first protest, Eberhard Baumann's, came to Superintendent Onnasch. This was not the first time that Baumann had been involved in controversies over Bonhoeffer's writings. As he was the avowed theological expert of the Stettin Council of Brethren, many expected him to put this young man right! When, in 1936, Friedrich Baumgärtel had attacked an article by Bonhoeffer in Junge Kirche, *Baumann had had to explain that such articles were not official pronouncements of the Confessing Church. Now it was the turn of Onnasch to tell Baumann that although the Pomeranian Council of Brethren circulated Bonhoeffer's theological supplement with their monthly letter to Pomeranian clergy these supplements were not to be regarded as theological statements of the Confessing Church. Bonhoeffer, however, soon came to his own defence in the letter quoted above.*

Bonhoeffer was controversial! And it was this controversy which kept the theological work of the Confessing Church alive.

'The theological commission very active with Bonhoeffer', wrote Frau Ohnesorge in January 1940. That was before the offensive February letter. Two further theological supplements will show that Bonhoeffer was leading the young clergy to think carefully about the basis of their faith. He was deeply concerned with affairs in Berlin and the proposed coup d'état *with which Dohnanyi was so much involved. He saw little point in the various peace-feelers and had lost confidence in the ecumenical movement. His main work at this time was not even with the Church Struggle. He saw that political action was needed and, on that front, Hitler had to be got rid of, but he also saw the importance for the Confessing Church of a clear theology. In March, he dealt with the resurrection, and in April, the ascension as the last resurrection appearance:*

THE MARCH THEOLOGICAL SUPPLEMENT: THE RESURRECTION

1. *The resurrection of Jesus Christ is God's 'Yes' to Christ and his redeeming work*
The cross was the end, the death of the Son of God, curse and

45

judgement upon all flesh. If the cross were the last word about Jesus, then the world would be lost in death and damnation, without hope, it would have been a victory over God. But God, who alone accomplished salvation for us, raised Christ from the dead. That was the new beginning, which followed the end as a miracle from above, not in accordance with a firm law, as spring follows winter, but because of the incomparable freedom and power of God, which shatters death. 'Scripture has proclaimed how one death devoured the other' (Luther). In this way God has acknowledged Jesus Christ; indeed, as the Apostle can say: the resurrection is the day on which the Son of God is begotten (Acts 13. 33; Rom. 1. 4). The Son receives back his eternal divine glory, the Father has the Son again. So Jesus is confirmed and glorified as the Christ of God which he was from the beginning. In this way, the representative, satisfactory work of Jesus Christ is acknowledged and accepted by God. Jesus uttered his cry of desolation on the cross and then commended himself to the hands of his Father, who was to make what he pleased of him and his work. In the resurrection of Jesus Christ, it has become certain that God has said 'Yes' to his Son and his work. So we hail the Risen One as the Son of God, the Lord and Saviour.

2. *The resurrection of Jesus Christ is God's 'Yes' to us*
Christ died for our sins, he was raised for our justification (Rom. 4. 25). Christ's death was the death sentence on us and our sins. If Christ had remained dead, this death sentence would still be in force, 'we would still be in our sins' (I Cor. 15. 17). But because Christ has been raised from the dead, the verdict on us is repealed, and we are risen with Christ (I Cor. 15). That is the case because by virtue of the acceptance of our human nature in the incarnation we are in Jesus Christ; what happened to him happens to us for we have been accepted by

him. That is no judgement of experience, but a verdict of God, which is to be recognized in faith in God's word.

3. *The resurrection of Jesus Christ is God's 'Yes' to all that he has made*

Not destruction, but a recreation of the body happens here. The body of Jesus emerges from the tomb and the tomb is empty. We cannot see how it is possible, how it is conceivable that the mortal and corruptible body is now the immortal, incorruptible, transfigured body. Nothing is perhaps so clear from the different character of the reports of the encounters of the Risen One with the disciples as the fact that we cannot picture the new body of the Risen One. We know that the body is the same – for the tomb is empty; and that it is a new body – for the tomb is empty. We know that God has judged the first creation and that he has made a new creation like the first. What survives is not an idea about Christ, but the bodily Christ himself. That is God's 'Yes' to the new creature in the midst of the old. In the resurrection we recognize that God has not abandoned the earth, but has taken it back to himself. He has given it a new future, a new promise. The same earth which God created bore the Son of God and his cross, and on this earth the Risen One appeared to his own, and to this earth Christ will return on the Last Day. Anyone who affirms the resurrection of Christ can no longer flee the world, nor can he fall victim to the world, for he has recognized the new creation of God in the midst of the old creation.

The resurrection of Jesus Christ demands faith. It is the unanimous testimony of all accounts, however different their reports of what happened and was experienced, that the Risen One did not show himself to the world, but only to his own (Acts 10. 40 ff.). Jesus does not display himself to an impartial authority, so as to let the miracle of his resurrection be authenticated before the world, and thus to compel recognition. He means to be believed, preached, and believed again. The world sees only the negative side, the earthly expression of the divine wonder. It sees the empty tomb and explains it (though in deliberate self-deception) as the pious mistake of the disciples (Matt. 28. 11 ff.); it sees the joy and the messages of the disciples and calls it all visions, auto-suggestion. The world sees the signs, but it does not believe the miracle. Only where the miracle is believed do the signs become divine signs and aids to faith. For the world the empty tomb is an ambiguous *historical* fact, for the faithful it is the *historic* sign of God, who acts in history with men, which necessarily follows from the miracle of the resurrection.

It is impossible to demonstrate the resurrection by historical method; even for the historian there are only a number of extremely odd facts which are impossible for him to interpret; for example, had the tomb not been empty, it would have been the strongest argument against a physical resurrection and indeed the basis of polemic against Christianity; on the other hand, we never find this objection; indeed the opposition itself confirms the empty tomb (Matt. 28. 11), and this is strengthened by the sudden change of circumstances two days after the crucifixion. Deliberate deception is psychologically excluded by the whole conduct of the disciples before and after, and also by the very inconsistency of the accounts of the resurrection. Self-deception by visions is ruled out as virtually impossible by the unprejudiced historian because of the initial unbelieving, sceptical rejection of the message by the disciples (Luke 24. 11, etc.), and also because of the varied character of the appearances. Thus the decision of the historian in this case, which scientifically remains so mysterious, will be dictated by the presuppositions of his particular approach. But in this way it loses interest and importance for a faith which is based on God's action in history.

So for the world there remains an insoluble riddle, which cannot in any way compel faith in the resurrection of Jesus. But to faith this riddle is a sign of the reality of which one already knows, an impress of the divine action in history. Scholarship can still neither prove nor disprove the resurrection of Jesus, for it is a miracle of God. But faith, to which the Risen One shows himself as being alive, recognizes precisely in the testimony of Scripture the historicity of the resurrection as an act of God which in its character as a miracle can present itself to scholarship only as a riddle. The certainty of the resurrection is received only by faith, from present testimony to Christ. It finds its confirmation in this historical impression made by the miracle, as it is reported by Scripture.

It is the grace of Jesus Christ that he still does not reveal himself visibly to the world, for the very moment at which that happened would be the end, and thus the judgement of unbelief. So the Risen One avoids any visible reinstatement before the world; for that would be judgement on the world. He is witnessed to in his community in his hidden glory, and he lets the word bear witness to him before all the world, until the Last Day, when he returns visibly to judge all men.

THE APRIL THEOLOGICAL SUPPLEMENT:
THE ASCENSION OF JESUS CHRIST
(A consideration of its christological, soteriological and parenetic significance)

A. CHRISTOLOGICAL

1. *The ascension of Jesus is the return of the Son of God to his origin*
Jesus enters the glory of the invisible God. He remains man for ever. His human nature, accepted in time, is taken up into

eternity. It has passed from a state of humiliation to a state of complete exaltation. The Lutheran Fathers emphatically distinguished between incarnation and humiliation. They said that it was not the *Logos asarkos*, but the *Logos ensarkos*, i.e. the incarnate Son of God, who is the 'subject of the incarnation'. In this way they gave honour and hope in God to the manhood created by God and assumed in Christ. The incarnate Son of God humbled himself and is exalted in the descent into hell, the resurrection and the ascension. When the human nature of Jesus Christ is freed from the state of humiliation it participates in the properties of the divine nature without concealment. What was real from the first moment of Christ's being a man, and still remained hidden in the state of humiliation, i.e. the permeation of the human nature by the properties of the divine nature, is manifested in the state of exaltation. The manhood that has been assumed, the man Jesus Christ, enters the eternity of the Father. But in order to be preserved here from philosophical speculation which finally merges the manhood and the Godhead, in other words, to oppose any mystical identity, the Lutheran Fathers taught that while the Son of God has his manhood eternally, the Son of God also remains in the complete communion of the triune God, while the manhood which was assumed, i.e. the human nature of Jesus Christ, is not itself taken up into the Trinity, but remains subordinate to it for ever; for manhood can never become Godhead; otherwise God would cease to be the Creator, Reconciler and Redeemer of mankind.

2. *The ascension is the last of the Easter appearances of the Lord*
Jesus physically entered the transfigured world of God through the resurrection. There is no difference between the mode of existence of the Risen One and that of the Ascended One, only in the mode of appearance. In the forty days Jesus showed

himself as the one who now remains for eternity the living, corporeal Lord, who has returned to the world of God (John 20. 17). This prevents us from declaring a difference between the body of the Risen One and that of the Ascended One (for here Jesus simply rejects Mary's mistaken idea that she could now touch him as she did before the crucifixion; in other words, he would not be remaining with her like this, but would return for ever and be with his own only after the ascension), nor can it be said that Jesus had a physical body after his resurrection (Thomas!) but not after his ascension; this would take no account of the appearance to Saul. Jesus' refusal to allow Mary to touch him, his permission to Thomas to touch the marks of his wounds, his appearance to Saul in a shining light of glory, only mean that Mary is to be saved from the error of a false love of Jesus, Thomas from doubt that what he saw was real, and Saul from his disbelief in the living Christ. But Jesus is the same in all instances. Paul puts the appearance of Jesus which is his call in the same series as the Easter appearances (I Cor. 15. 1 ff.). It is the same risen Christ who called him to belong among the witnesses of his resurrection (cf. also Acts 7. 56; 18. 9; 22. 7). Nevertheless, the forty days between Easter and Ascension are of decisive significance. They include the new call and the sending out of the witnesses in the service of the Risen One. The office of proclaiming the gospel depends on the forty days. That is the unanimous testimony of Scripture (Mark 16. 15 ff.; Matt. 28. 18 ff.; John 20. 22 ff.; Acts 1. 8; 10. 42). But Jesus remains forty days with his followers not for his sake but for theirs. Because in his case the resurrection represents no alteration of his mode of being. Scripture can often call the resurrection of Jesus the decisive act without mentioning the ascension (Rom. 1. 3 ff.; Acts 10. 41; 13. 31, etc., but see Acts 2. 33; 3. 21, etc.). From this point of view the ascension of Jesus simply represents the end of his appearances on earth, although even then Christ remains free in his influence (Acts 9. 5).

3. *The ascension is the exaltation of Jesus to the right hand of God*
The sign of being raised into the clouds merely means that from now on Jesus will be wholly in the world of God. But that does not permit any sort of speculation about the place where he now dwells. If Scripture wants to say that Jesus is no longer in the world of men, but in the world of God, it expresses this with the simple expression that Jesus has gone 'to heaven' (Heb. 9. 24; Eph. 1. 20). But if Scripture wants to exclude any conceivable approach which would still confine Jesus to the created world, it says more sharply: he has ascended above all the heavens, he has passed through the heavens, he has become higher than the heavens (Eph. 4. 10; Heb. 4. 14; 7. 26). Sitting on the right hand of God, Jesus participates in God's rule of the world; he is far from the world and at the same time as near as God himself. Any idea which would keep Jesus bound to a particular place because of his body goes beyond these biblical expressions. Acts 3. 21 also simply says that Christ is now in heaven and has not yet come again, but that does not exclude the divine omnipresence of Jesus Christ, who sits at the right hand of God. Anyone who asks how Jesus, despite his bodiliness, can participate in the divine omnipresence, must equally ask how the spiritual body of Jesus could have eaten and drunk, and allowed itself to be touched, in the days after Easter. All that is revealed to us is that Jesus Christ has been raised with a transfigured body to the glory of the Father and participates in his power, his distance, and his presence.

B. SOTERIOLOGICAL

1. *The ascension is the proclamation of Jesus as lord of the world and head of the Church*
The proof of the 'mighty power' of God is that he has made Jesus 'sit at his right hand in the heavenly places, far above all rule and authority and power and dominion, and above every name that is named, not only in this age, but also in that which is to come' (Eph. 1. 20). Christ has succeeded to the rule of the world. Fate, authorities, powers are in his hand. There is no account of an ascension in Matthew. Jesus' last words in Matthew 28. 18 take its place: 'All authority in heaven and on earth has been given to me. . . . and lo, I am with you always, to the close of the age'; that is the ascension message itself. The wonder is attested, only the sign remains unmentioned. Now Christ exercises his kingly office – as the Fathers called it – to his full extent. The king of all the world is at the same time the head of the Church. The head is in heaven, the body is on earth. The invisible head rules the visible body. So the heavenly Christ is still fully present on earth, he fills his community, and with it and through it all in all (Eph. 1. 23); for through the Church he gradually permeates the whole world which belongs to him and fills it with his effective presence. As the one who has been to the depths of hell and to the heights of heaven, as the one who has passed through all this in divine power and fills all things, he can now also give the community the divine gifts which it needs (Eph. 4. 8 ff.); he gives it the offices which authoritatively call the world to God and believers to Christ. The Lord who has been taken away into the distance of the transfigured world of God has in this way become all the nearer to the world and the Church.

2. 'Christ has entered . . . into heaven itself, now to appear in the presence of God on our behalf' (Heb. 9. 24)

That is the consummation of his priestly office. Because he bore all our sins on the cross, he can now be our intercessor (I John 2. 1), and our prayers, which would otherwise ring out in emptiness, are brought by him to the Father and find a hearing. Only in the name of Jesus can we pray. For Christ, as high priest, has reconciled us to God and offers his sacrifice in intercession for us before God to all eternity. The Fathers called that the *intercessio Christi* (Rom. 8. 34; John 14. 16; Heb. 4. 14) and wanted to apply this priestly action of the exalted Lord not only to believers but also to unbelievers 'so that they too may have the fruits of his saving death' (Hollaz).

3. *Just as Christ went to heaven, so one day he will return again from heaven for judgement*

We thus recognize the exalted Lord as the future judge, for whom we must wait. He is still hidden, that is his patience; for faith can still find grace in him. But when he returns visible, the day of judgement will have come.

C. PARENETIC

1. *The ascension of Jesus summons us to faith, to confession, to worship*

Because God has raised Jesus and has given him heavenly glory, we have faith and hope in God (I Peter 1. 21). Because our high priest is not an earthly man, but the Son of God, who has gone to heaven, we hold firm to our confession of him as our salvation (Heb. 4. 14). Because Jesus is immeasurably exalted above us, we worship him (Luke 24. 52).

2. *The ascension of Jesus has raised us to heavenly places* (*Eph. 2. 6*)
and thus directs our gaze to heaven (*Col. 3. 1*)
Just as we died with Christ in his body and rose again (Col.
2. 12), so we are also raised with him into the heavenly places.
This exalted, unique, assertion of the Epistle to the Ephesians
teaches us to be reconciled in and with the Lord who has
ascended into heaven, as those who are always with him in the
power of the manhood which he has taken. Where he is, there
we are too. We are already in heaven with Christ. But, for
that very reason, we seek and look for what is above. 'They
walk on earth and live in heaven', runs the hymn. The future
is present and the present is already past. So we live in the
power of Christ's ascension.

3. *The ascension of Jesus puts us between having and waiting*
We have heaven, and so we wait for it. We are raised into the
heavenly places, our citizenship is in heaven (Phil. 3. 20), and
we ask for the return of the Lord from heaven. Those who
wait watch and make themselves ready for the day of joy
(Matt. 24. 43 ff., etc). The final appearance of Jesus will,
however, transfigure the community of believers into the glory
of the Lord and take them for ever into the heavenly kingdom.

G.S. III pp. 405–15

*Here we appear to have Bonhoeffer completely absorbed in his
theology and the instruction of his young pastors. Even an important
conference on 'The Church's Responsibility for International Order',
which was held in Berlin in April, under the sponsorship of the
World Council of Churches (in process of formation), failed to
attract his attention. He was in Berlin at the time and the conference
was attended by leading ecumenical figures, many of whom he must
have known from his earlier work. Yet he neither referred to it nor*

visited it! Clearly, Bonhoeffer had little sympathy with its views on 'international order'. It may have been the other sponsoring body that kept him away from it – the German Church's External Affairs Office!

2. The Logic of Events

No one could deny the influence of events upon Bonhoeffer's thinking. In May 1940 we see the author of The Cost of Disciple-ship *strongly influenced in his application of theology by the events of the war. It was at that time that he addressed a letter to his young pastors on military service:*

May 1940

BONHOEFFER TO THE BRETHREN: Today for once I must send you all a combined word of thanks for the greetings and letters which I've had from you recently. I couldn't cope with writing to you otherwise, and I don't want you to have to wait any longer for my thanks. Each greeting and each long letter has given me great delight, and has made it possible for me to adjust my ideas better about individuals. But you mustn't think that I want to make further claims on the little free time which you have and need for your families and yourselves. I can imagine that with all one's experiences one sometimes doesn't want to speak and write about them any more, particularly when one is already writing home. In that case, I really don't want to extort any letters from you. I often feel ashamed when I get a long letter from the front. I sometimes think then that the person who wrote it could certainly have done with his sleep and his rest. I needn't say that I enjoy every greeting from a really free hour. Thank you for all your sacrifices of time and rest which you have made to write your letters.

Many of you want to hear more of how things are going here, so that we don't lose contact. I can well understand that. But you must remember that it's a consequence of the times in which we live that each person must be content to be able to do his duty in his place. One often loses most of the wider perspective. Sad as that is, it also has its good points; now is a time of testing for the individual, to see whether he can do his work faithfully by himself for a time. We still don't know how it will work out, but as far as I can see, I haven't the impression that the whole thing is suffering damage because of it. Anyone who has learnt so far what is at stake is standing fast, even if he has to stand alone for a while, as long as it is not for too long. The greatest difficulty at the moment, and I think that you will agree, is the question of replacements. All conceivable avenues really have been explored here. In some places it is almost beyond the resources of the brethren. But where we then come up so clearly against the limits of our service, we shouldn't be worried to death by scruples. Prayer, and faith, and thankfulness for what we can still do, fill the gap here. It doesn't seem to me to be right to burden the individual inwardly and outwardly with particular worries. Most people have enough to put up with. Each one must know how he is fighting his way through his tasks with God's word, and there he can be certain of the intercession of the brethren and the power of Jesus Christ.

It is, I think, time once again to say something about the freedom of our Christian life and of the grace of God. Some of you who are in the field write in a state of depression about the difficulty of combining an ordered Christian life with the daily work which occupies the whole of your time. Many people simply cannot find time and peace for the reading of the Bible, for prayer and for intercession. In addition, the possibilities of having the sort of conversations that we long for as Christians, and of exercising a degree of influence on the general topics of conversation seem to vary from place to place. Some write very happily about this, others are equally troubled. I don't know now whether it is quite right to keep writing to you and telling you that even at the front you are and must be 'in the ministry'. Certainly none of us is ever released from the responsibility of being a Christian and no one may deny that he is a pastor. But isn't that rather different from saying so obviously that even at the front one is 'in the ministry'? In my view, you are not, and in that position you really cannot be. I'm afraid here of an illusion which will become a harsh law for the serious ones in particular, against which they will chafe and by which in the end they will be broken. Perhaps you say that your ordination itself laid this law upon you. I won't discuss the theological questions of ordination here, and their significance for the person who for some reason cannot exercise his ministry (for example, in a change of profession). Opinions differ here. But one thing is certain: ordination has been appointed as a comfort and a grace for us, to make us certain in our ministry. It is not meant to trouble us, so that we have our doubts about it, and in any case it will certainly not do that to you now. I think I ought to say that once again. In this matter we must be very careful about enthusiastic thoughts which are perhaps very fine for a while but may one day be very dangerous for us and lead our whole faith astray. One of you writes in some distress that he can only be a soldier among soldiers and that in so doing he is trying to remain a Christian, but that he has no strength for more than this. I would like to reassure him and all who feel the same. I cannot see any unfaithfulness towards one's ministry in this. One simply cannot continue to lead a pastor's life as a soldier, and one should not tear oneself apart inside trying to do so. Of course it's splendid if one's military service leaves one as much time as one needs for God's word. But whether that is the case or not, most of you are no longer responsible for it. Of course it is cheering to be able to have some influence and to help in conversations. But the limits which are appointed here are certainly not set by our own failings alone. Of course it would be fine if we were able to exercise some influence on certain words that are spoken and on conversations that go on around us. But I don't believe that it is good or advisable to cultivate too great a sensibility in oneself – that perhaps will only make us weak and unable to give any substantial help. Anyone who has learnt in the cross of Jesus Christ to know the power and character of the world and his own wickedness, and who at the same time seriously believes in the infinite love of God for this world, should no longer be too surprised or shaken by certain expressions of this worldliness. Anyway, I hope you understand what I mean. We rejoice with anyone for whom doors have been opened, and with them we give thanks to God, but we also stand alongside anyone with whom things are different, and we would not want them to be misled about their call to the ministry.

The great difference between your existence, my dear brothers in the field, and ours, who still have freedom for our ministry, is that we can put ourselves in a place which in a certain sense we have chosen for ourselves, freely, through our profession, whereas you now share the life of millions of people who have never been free in this sense because of the conditions governing their life and work. The inner change associated with that is probably the most difficult thing of all for us, and sometimes it even makes it no longer easy for us to understand one another.

Apart from all the Christian problems, this deep change in our life certainly also brings with it the need to rearrange our life with the word of God. Your life hitherto has been determined by a different measure of the consciousness of being a Christian from that which obtains at present. Whereas in our ministry we are reminded hourly of our status as Christians, hours and whole days pass for you without your being left a moment for such reminiscences, just as happens with the majority of working men. If the moment of recollection, which cannot hold off, comes then, in the morning or in the evening, or at an unexpected hour, it is probably so over-powering that we are hardly able to stand up to it. So we long all the more for that abiding communion with the word of God which we had in our ministry. And then it can also come about that we make false accusations against ourselves, that we look for a firm routine of Christian life which we cannot have at the time. We do indeed know that order and the conscious-ness of one's Christian existence is a good and generally helpful thing, but nevertheless it is not everything. The sudden, harsh clash of daily work and the word of God, which you certainly often experience now, must at times take the place of a regular discipline. We should not let ourselves be made slaves. God knows your present life and finds his way to you even in the most tense, the busiest days, if you can no longer find your way to him.

But now for once let's stop looking at our different situations and tasks and thinking about them, and let's look together at *God's* work, which does not stand still, whether we are this way or that, at his work in us, in his Church, and in the whole world. Let's look at his grace, which has preserved us so far through many dark hours, when we were worried about what might happen. Let's look at his faithfulness, which has still always been constant. God has begun with us and our Church, and he will also carry things through to the end, so that all will be well for everyone. May the Lord Jesus Christ keep us in his grace to the end.

The meditation texts have been chosen this time particularly for the sake of the brothers in the field, to match the sayings for the week, and for a longer time in advance. If for any reason a further edition of texts is impossible, we will always stay near to the sayings for the week. Once again I would draw your attention to the small edition of the Stuttgart Jubilee Bible, which, with its notes on the text and content, makes the reading, particularly of the Old Testament, sometimes very much easier, especially when one has no other help handy.

Dear brothers at home, perhaps you feel that this letter has said too little to you. But we cannot do our work without thinking incessantly of our brothers at the front and sending our thoughts after them, and it is just the same for those out there. How soon everything can change for us, too! Until then, be glad in your work, and thankful for each new day in which God still lets you serve the communities. Let us pray for one another, that we may rightly bear the responsibility laid upon us and be true shepherds of the communities. Our Church was founded through the Holy Spirit at Pentecost. The Holy Spirit will also sustain it. May God, the Holy Spirit, fill all our hearts with new love for his word, for his community, for all men. God bless you, your homes and your communities. G.S. II pp. 564–9

His pastoral concern for the brethren had already led him to see that under the conditions of military service a different discipline applies. The young men of the Confessing Church were not chaplains and they are each being urged to accept their role as 'a soldier among soldiers'. Bonhoeffer is already querying whether he should write to them telling them they are still 'in the ministry'. While he still has freedom for his ministry, they share the lot of most Christians 'who have never been free in this sense because of the conditions governing their life and work'.

A few months later in writing for Advent 1940 Bonhoeffer shows clearly that the war conditions are not exceptions, to pass one day. They in fact reveal more clearly the nature of the world in which we witness, 'like a speeded-up film'.[1]

Relations between the State and the Church were improving and state officials were discouraged from interfering too much in the affairs of the Church. But there were interferences. Bethge quotes a very interesting letter of protest by a serving soldier against these interferences in his biography of Bonhoeffer.[2] Bethge also gives details of some which led to great difficulties for the Confessing Church. Arrests and call-ups hindered the work of the Councils of Brethren. There were other petty annoyances and always the rumours of euthanasia and deportation of Jews, which kept the Confessing Church constantly aware of the true enemy. Pastor Grüber protested against the transportation of Jews from Stettin and was warned. Bonhoeffer took the same line and was known to be 'radical'. During June 1940 he wrote from Königsberg:

I find Königsberg to be a town in which a man can live well, unlike Stettin. But behind everything that one sees stands the spectre of other events . . .   G.S.II p. 373

Those other events may well be the German entry into Paris, the appeal for an armistice by Pétain and the French capitulation, all in June; but it was from Stettin that the Jews first began that ghastly episode of transportation. In July he is travelling still in the same area:

I go today to Danzig, then to Frau von Kleist and should be in Berlin for Monday and Tuesday, where I must talk with Hans . . .   G.S.II p. 374

He had fallen foul of the Gestapo on 13th July and from that point on he needed the protection of Hans von Dohnanyi. A study con-

---

[1] See page 78.   [2] p. 591.

ference which he had arranged with former students at Blöstau was dissolved on 14th July and Bonhoeffer protested. It was probably in connection with this that he was later, in September, forbidden to speak in public and required to report regularly to the police. With these clouds gathering he had talks with Oster and Dohnanyi about extra-parochial duties, which would allow him to work with the Abwehr. The years of conspiracy were about to begin. A little of this is seen in the letter by which he protested against the prohibition to speak in public, a letter addressed to the office of the Minister of National Security in Berlin:

On 9th September, 1940, the State Police Headquarters at Köslin informed me of the National Security Office order IV A 4g 776/40 by which I am prohibited from speaking in public in the territory of the Reich. The reason given is 'disruptive activity'. I reject this charge. In view of my whole attitude, my work and my background, it is unthinkable that I should allow myself to be identified with groups which rightly bear the ignominy of such a charge. I am proud to belong to a family which has for generations earned the gratitude of the German people and state. Among my ancestors are General Field-Marshal Count Kalckreuth and the two great German painters of the same name, the Church historian Karl von Hase of Jena, well known throughout the academic world of the last century; and the Cauer family, the sculptors. Lieutenant General Graf von der Goltz, who liberated the Baltic, is my uncle, and his son, Staatsrat Rüdiger Graf von der Goltz, is my first cousin. Lieutenant General von Hase, who is on active service, is also my uncle. For almost thirty years my father has been Ordinarius Professor of Medicine in Berlin and still holds distinguished public appointments; for centuries his ancestors have been highly respected craftsmen and councillors of what was once the free city of Schwäbisch-

Hall, and their portraits are still proudly displayed in the city church there. My brothers and brothers-in-law have senior public appointments; one of my brothers was killed in the World War. It has been the concern of all these men and their families to serve the German state and its people at all times, and to risk their lives in its service. In deliberate affirmation of this spiritual heritage and this inward attitude of my family, I cannot accept the charge of 'disruptive activity'. Any conduct which could be described by this charge is alien to my nature, and is, so far as I am concerned, quite out of the question.

My personal work consists predominantly of academic research. I seldom take a public part in church affairs, and then almost always by way of academic theological lectures. So far there has never been any official criticism of anything that I have said. I consider it my task in the German Evangelical Church to see that academic work continues undisturbed and that a high quality of research is maintained, and for my own part to contribute towards keeping German scholarship in high repute.

I have been informed that 'lectures', which I am said to have given to a 'part-time course for theological students' have led to this prohibition. My explanation of this is as follows:

On the occasion of a stay in East Prussia, I was invited to take a Bible study and to give a lecture for a small meeting of Königsberg students of different faculties. Three or four students met at Blöstau, near Königsberg, on 13th July, 1940, and there were about as many members of the congregation. In the afternoon I took a Bible study, followed by a short talk about the gospel story of the rich young ruler. I append the outline of the Bible study. On the Sunday morning, I conducted worship for the Blöstau congregation and preached on the gospel for the day. After the service I was sitting and talking for a short time with three or four students when a considerable number of officials of the Secret Police appeared and told us that we must disperse. Our attention was drawn to an order of the end of June 1940 which none of us knew about, as it had never been published, and which was not even produced for us despite our constant requests, according to which the prohibition of part-time meetings for Christian Youth was also to apply to adults of 'Confessional organizations'. One of the officials told me himself that I had nothing more to worry about as they were only carrying out orders as a matter of routine. Another said that they would not have come had they known that there were only four or five people in the group. With this, the meeting ended. What objection could be made to my remarks, I do not know. I only know that I dealt exclusively with religious and pastoral questions, which had nothing in the least to do with 'disruptive activity'. Clearly I am available to provide any further information or to discuss the matter. I am also convinced that just a short conversation would make it clear that there is some misunderstanding here and that the charge of an objectionable piece of political conduct on my part cannot be sustained. I could easily explain what I was doing in East Prussia. When I was preaching there, in a number of communities, I was helping some pastors who are on active service, so that they would have the certainty and assurance that their communities were being cared for in their absence; I also did it to help the communities of the homeland, so that they would not feel neglected during the absence of their pastors. The Secret Police did not make the slightest complaint about any of these sermons.

May I now ask for an opportunity to discuss this, or at least that you should tell me whether I am also to be prevented, through this prohibition, from presenting the results of my wholly non-political academic activity to small groups? To give an example, may I talk to, say, between twenty and thirty interested hearers about the attitude of Luther to this or that question of Christian belief? I cannot believe that the prohibition is meant to be interpreted in this sense. I therefore ask you to allow me at least this activity. *Heil Hitler!* G.S.II pp. 363–6

This letter remained unanswered. He had now to make up his mind about his future occupation. He went away to Klein-Krössin and worked hard for four weeks on the early chapters of his Ethics. *This was on the estate of Frau von Kleist, mentioned in the July letter. He waited there while arrangements were made for him to be put on the staff of the* Abwehr *at Munich. His prohibition in Pomerania made difficulties for him, because while he was there he would have to report regularly to the police. He spent October at Klein-Krössin and then reported to the Munich office. For a considerable part of the rest of the year Bonhoeffer was at the Benedictine abbey of Ettal in Bavaria and there his thought developed, as is shown by the following letters written towards the end of 1940 from various places:*

Klein-Krössin, 9th October, 1940

BONHOEFFER TO BETHGE: Tomorrow, when you come home, you ought to have at least a greeting from me. You're now leading a much more active and, on the whole, much richer life than I am; but you mustn't let your energy be sapped by it. Keep your independence as much as possible. I feel that much of the weariness and sterility in our ranks is in the end a result of a lack of 'selfless self-love'. As this *locus* has no place in official evangelical ethics, people in their pride and their craze for work ignore it, to the loss of the individual and the whole. But it is a part of the human life for which we have been redeemed. So tell yourself that at the right time. I enjoy the daily morning prayers here very much: they make me expound the Bible. I think about you and your work a great deal during them, as I do when reading the Bible. The regular routine of the day makes it easy for me to work and to pray, and to get on with people, and it spares me the discomforts of body, soul and spirit that come from inactivity. Recently, however, a heavy autumn storm made me quite depressed, and it was not so easy to get my balance again. Work goes on: I'm doing an outline of the whole thing [i.e. his *Ethics*] which is the task I always enjoy most and find most difficult. It will probably take the rest of the week.

We were in Kieckow on Sunday. We also talked about the church situation. Once again it became quite clear to me that the struggle over the government of the Church is in fact *the* question, which has inevitably arisen out of the history of the Church, the question of the possibility of a 'protestant' Church for us. It is the question whether, after the split between papal and secular authority in the Church, an authority can be appointed in the Church which is based solely on the Word and the Confessions. If such an authority is not possible, then the last possibility for a 'protestant' Church has gone; in that case, all that is left is a return to Rome, or to the state Church, or a way into isolation, into the 'protest' of true Protestantism against false authorities. Our present concern with the authority of the government of the Church is not fortuitous, but a divine necessity.

My thoughts are often turning to Sabine . . . When one has the feeling that others expected something of one and that one has fallen so far short of their expectations, one's memory is filled with a sense of guilt and at the same time a desire for forgiveness and to be able to help again . . . How's the economic situation? And the air-raid shelters? There was an alert again today in Köslin. All the best. See you next week.

G.S.II pp. 375–7

The Benedictine abbey at Ettal was to be his home and study for a long time. On 31st October he visited briefly to make future arrange-

ments. During that brief visit he wrote to Bethge. It was the day following his appointment to the Abwehr *office in Munich:*

BONHOEFFER TO BETHGE: Arrived yesterday with a four-hour delay in Munich; a most lively day with a number of people. Today a short visit up here, where I have been invited later on. This evening back to Munich for two more days to meet still more people. It is a most splendid winter up here. I hope you can get here. More soon. Best wishes, in haste . . .

G.S.II p. 377

A few days later, Bonhoeffer writes from a hotel in Munich and his plans are far from clear. But he is finding co-operation with Catholics stimulating:

Park Hotel, Munich, 4th November, 1940

BONHOEFFER TO BETHGE: . . . I expect you're in the thick of preparations for Bible Week. A pity that we can't prepare it together once again. I'm trying to get a foothold in the circles here which interest me; I think it will be easier with the other Confession than with our own people! Anyway, it is already clear that all the necessary contacts have so far been completely lacking. I'm now visiting a great many people and discussing these things. Great agitation in the Ordinariate today: a ban on book-stalls in the churches; pre-military training arranged for Sunday, 8 a.m.–11 a.m.; after an air-raid, no service before 10 a.m., no bells before one. These three things came all at once and produced a very perceptible echo, and also a great deal of open criticism of the bishops. My plans are now as follows: if I get no news tomorrow (Tuesday) about my return to Berlin, I will ring up home in the evening (please tell them), so that I can make more arrangements about my time here. I hope that things will straighten themselves out after my visits today and tomorrow. I've often been to the theatre in the evenings – I've seen *Ariadne* and

Otello, and today I'm going to a Bach concert. Just think, I've found two hundred marks in a side-pocket of my brief-case. Won't we need them for the Christmas trip? Or shall I send you something very splendid? Half is yours anyway. More soon. Now I'm going to see my publisher. A full day after that. I'm thinking of you and your work.   G.S.II pp. 377–8

A few days later from Berlin:

BONHOEFFER TO BETHGE: Greetings again in haste before I go. I'm off tomorrow to Jena to talk to Staemmler. Write soon, to Munich, 'Europäischer Hof'. God bless you.

G.S.II p. 378

On the train back to Munich, he shares his plans again with Bethge:

16th November, 1940

BONHOEFFER TO BETHGE: I'm sitting in the train to Munich and have just been thoroughly disillusioned. The train doesn't arrive at 8.30, as I thought, but at 10.30. I can't read any more, so I'm writing an illegible letter to you.

The visit to Staemmler was very good. He began with his conversation with you, in which you evidently put my case in a touching and friendly way, with the happy result that they now all have a bad conscience about me. I certainly didn't intend that, but in any case it was very nice of you to set things rolling. They have therefore decided that I can continue as head of the training centre of the Confessing Church and keep myself in readiness, but that until then I should do some academic work. Staemmler was very sceptical about a pastorate. He was not very keen on Bismarck [a parish in Altmark]. So for the moment, I am free. And with a clear conscience that they want it this way. What shall I do now? If I am really free for at least five months, it is not very good to live in an hotel. But what then? Hire a small place in the hills? And have some of the books sent? The von Rads have a small house (with central heating) to let in the neighbourhood of the Chiemsee, thirty to forty marks a month, furnished, several rooms. That sounds attractive. But very lonely in the long run. I must still see what the military position is. And in the end it mustn't be Bavaria. How splendid it would be if we could do something together! Can you think of a solution? Von Rad will visit me at Ettal in December. When are you coming? You could visit Neuendettelsau again and go to take a look at the Catholic 'Volksmission', perhaps also go on to Austria. Discuss that some time with Lokies. Or shall I write to him? As you like. Staemmler was very nice personally. We also spoke about Catholic affairs, very reasonably. Asmussen is said to have preached at a *Una Sancta* service. I think that is going too far. He has no stability . . . I exchanged reminiscences with von Rad. He is very lonely, and after eighteen years I like him very much again. He seems to me to be quite clear about the Church – Staemmler asked whether you were coming. When I said 'Yes', he said quite quietly, 'Ah, that's very good'. He also needs support and help. On the other hand, you yourself have plenty of other things to do. Think about my advice on self-love.

One more word about the Catholic question: How have we Lutherans got along with the Reformed Churches? Really quite untheologically (the theological formulation of Halle is really more a statement of fact than a theological solution). We have managed to work together on the basis of two things: the 'guidance' of God (Union, Confessing Church) and the recognition of what is given objectively in the sacraments: Christ is more important than our thoughts about him and his presence. Both are theologically questionable foundations for unity, and yet the Church decided in faith for eucharistic – i.e. inter-Church – communion. It decided to recognize the union as the guiding hand of God, and it decided to subordinate its ideas or doctrine about Christ to the objectivity of the presence of Christ (in the Reformed Eucharist, too). But it did not bring about a theological union (except at Halle). Would not these two things also be possible with respect to the Catholic Church? Recognition of the 'guidance' of God in recent years, recognition of the objectivity of the presence of Christ (easier for the old Lutherans in the case of the Catholics than in that of the Reformed Church!). It seems to me that Churches have united, not primarily theologically, but through decisions of faith, in the sense that I have mentioned. That's a very dangerous statement, isn't it! One can do anything with it! But have we in the Confessing Church not in fact done just that? Of course, the guidance was much clearer then. I don't think it can happen in a day or two, but I want to keep my eyes open in that direction. The train is jolting too much now. Excuse the shaking. Remember me to all old friends in Jena. Write to me at Ettal, via Oberau (Bavaria), Hotel Ludwig der Bayer.

G.S.II pp. 379–81

Once he had settled at the Benedictine abbey, he wrote to outline his plans to Bethge.

Ettal, 18th November, 1940

BONHOEFFER TO BETHGE: I've been here since yesterday – a most friendly welcome; eat in the refectory, sleep at the hotel, can use the library, have my own key to the cloister, had a good long chat with the abbot yesterday, in short, everything one could want. All I need is the desk! Many changes have taken place in my attitude to Catholics over the last six years . . . Further to my invitation for you to come here I just want to say that I have the best personal contacts with the greatest of the Catholic mission societies (Steyler Mission in Vienna) and that I have had the most pressing invitation to go there.

Wouldn't that justify a visit from you? I find that the people are open and ready so that I could imagine a fruitful conversation between you. I could take you with me without any difficulty, and I can easily make contact with the Catholic 'Volksmission'. I think that it would be interesting for you and that it would perhaps be quite opportune to take advantage of something like this. I am not sure how long I shall be here, so come in December! Tell Lokies that I think it important that these contacts should be made now. It would of course also be interesting for you here. So I hope that you will come. Let me know soon!   G.S.II pp. 381–2

Bonhoeffer wrote also to his parents, somewhat differently, a few days later:

Kloster Ettal, 21st November, 1940

BONHOEFFER TO HIS PARENTS: . . . I'm a guest here (which is not a good thing in the long run!), I live in the hotel, eat at the monastery, have access to the library, and get everything that I need. This sort of life isn't strange to me, and I find the regularity and silence very conducive to work. It would indeed be a loss (and it certainly was a loss at the Reformation) if this form of common life, which has been preserved for fifteen hundred years, should be destroyed, as is thought quite possible here. I think that a great deal of friction, which must inevitably be felt in such a close and permanent life together, is avoided through strict discipline. This provides a very sound basis for work. Some things are really strange, as for instance when historical works are read at lunch and supper in the singing tone of the liturgy; it is sometimes difficult to keep from laughing, particularly if the content is humorous. Otherwise I find the reading in such a large group not at all bad. I also introduced it at the seminary. In the course of time one gets acquainted with all sorts of things. Moreover, the food is

excellent. I'm now waiting for Christel and the children . . .
A great many people have been called up just now. Why, in
the winter?   G.S.II p. 382

A little later, when he had organized his work better, Bonhoeffer
explained to Bethge his changing attitude to the Catholics:

Ettal, Sunday, 23rd November, 1940

BONHOEFFER TO BETHGE: I'm glad, despite everything, that
you're now so fully occupied and can really do something
which is necessary that takes up all your time. My state of
retirement, on the other hand, seems so superfluous; but
there's no harm in feeling useless for a while. There's no
question about it, at present you are indispensable and that will
give you – 'penultimate' – satisfaction . . . I sometimes think
that the whole business (if it *is* unavoidable) can be a form of
cold storage for the future. But of course, how incomparably
easy and pleasant our life has been over the past few years,
when one considers the burdens which others have borne for
years. And what right would I have to quarrel, even for a
moment, with my situation, which for others would be a
foretaste of paradise! So please do not think that I am abandon-
ing myself without restraint to resignation; I already know and
tell myself every morning and every evening what I have to be
thankful for. – I've just come from a quite marvellous mass.
With *Schott* in one's hand one can still pray a great deal and be
utterly affirmative. It's not simply idolatry, even if I find the
way from our own sacrifice for God to God's sacrifice for us,
with which the mass is concerned, a hard and apparently very
perverse one. But I must learn to understand it better. I'm still
a guest over there. The ordered life suits me very well, and
I'm surprised at the similarity to much of what we did of our
own accord at the seminary. Moreover, the abbot and a
number of the fathers have read *Life Together*. We're going to

have a discussion soon. The natural hospitality, which is evidently something specifically Benedictine, the really Christian respect for strangers for Christ's sake, almost makes one ashamed. You should come here some time! It's a real experience . . .

Otherwise all goes well in body and spirit. I'm longing for a Eucharist. Recently, by mistake, I went to a Lutheran service of penitence in Munich. But the questions were so fearfully legalistic that I was quite glad not to be invited to the Eucharist. It was not much better than a mass. And in Meiser's church . . . ! Now goodbye, dear Eberhard. In the peace of my present abode I'm thinking a great deal about the brethren, the Confessing Church, you and your work.

Today the Pope has ordered prayers for peace throughout the Church. Couldn't we have joined them too? I did.

G.S.II pp. 383–4

Meanwhile, his work proceeded:

Ettal, 27th November, 1940

BONHOEFFER TO BETHGE: . . . Today I've thought of a possible title for my book: *Wegbereitung und Einzug (Preparing the Way and Entering Upon It)*, corresponding to the two parts of the book (the things before the last and the last things). What do you think of it? But don't bother yourself with questions like that. You've enough else . . . G.S.II p. 384

Ettal, 28th November, 1940

BONHOEFFER TO BETHGE: As I still keep waiting, I want to send you at least a greeting a day. If in the meanwhile it has turned out that you have to leave on Monday (and from your silence I suppose that I have to fear the worst), then I can at least be with you by letter. It seems quite unnatural for me not to be able to help you. At the moment all sorts of incidental things are going through my head. You mustn't forget to use

75

the clothing coupons for some more woollen clothing. I don't remember you having much woollen stuff, and you will certainly need it. Of course, I can give you all sorts of things of mine if you can no longer get them in Berlin. There's still a good variety in Munich. For the rest, if I were you I should buy another suit. I can let you have some more money. I've saved a great deal this month. Take some cigarettes, etc., too. Now I'm going to Munich, where I want to get something for the brothers for Christmas; then I'm meeting Hans. – Work goes on gradually. It's been a great festival today; anniversary of the consecration of the abbot, with processions and festival food. Very nice. I would have liked to tell you all about it face to face. Christmas at the latest. . . .   G.S.II p. 385

Ettal, 28th November, 1940

BONHOEFFER TO BETHGE: Just as I was leaving the hotel, your card arrived with the good news. Why didn't you send a telegram? Out of stinginess? I'll send you my telephone bills! Well, I'm very glad, and am curious to hear more . . .

G.S.II p. 385

Munich, 29th November, 1940

BONHOEFFER TO BETHGE: I've been in Munich since yesterday evening and among other things I've done my Christmas shopping . . . For my godchildren, the picture on the other side, bigger, and in a frame (Lochner's *Nativity*). I thought of the same thing for the Blocks and Frau Martin, to whom I always send something; perhaps this time you will take it over for me . . . In addition, I bought a hundred postcards with the Altdorfer, on the other card (Albrecht Altdorfer's *Nativity*). I find this picture very appropriate: Christmas among the ruins. I would like to send Furche's *Calvin's Letters to the Huguenots*. Most impressive. I will have to travel as soon as possible. How long for, I don't know. An interesting and unique job. Today

I saw the 'Volksmission' man here; very interesting, and really objective praise for you. Partly as in Finkenwalde, but also quite new ideas. You ought to know that. It's done here, and in the towns too. I don't know whether you have any other contacts here. We must arrange something as soon as my journey's fixed. Tell that to Lokies!

I still don't know for how long you are free. But it is without doubt a great privilege. I feel that very strongly; it's a real reprieve. The important thing is that we use it rightly, so that after it is over people will know how it was used . . . Now you can still have Advent and Christmas and work. I shall miss the hymns very much, quite apart from the preaching; we still had this at the seminary. I am all the more pleased for you that you can be in Finkenwalde now. They will be particularly grateful there. I wish you *parrēsia* and *sophrosynē* (boldness of speech and wisdom), and I shall be with you daily in my thoughts.

I don't find it physically easy to stand this hill country. The impenetrability of it sometimes lies like a burden even on one's work. Is 'Gebirge' ('hill') really connected with 'bergen' ('hide, shelter')? Sometimes I think so and feel it, but only rarely.

G.S.II pp. 386–7

After the dissolution of the 'collective pastorates' at Köslin and Sigurdshof, Bonhoeffer had kept in touch with his young pastors by means of a series of circular letters. While at Ettal, he wrote in this personal vein, not only to Bethge, but also to the younger men. He encouraged them to think their way through the difficult days of war and began to compare the impact of this war with 'the World War' through which he had lived as a boy. His letter for Christmas 1940 was particularly important for this:

Advent 1940

BONHOEFFER TO THE BRETHREN: When war broke out in 1914, it was regarded as an unparalleled turning point. A whole way of thinking and living was overturned, and something completely new took its place. Now this new element which the World War brought did not give way to the old, the 'pre-war', atmosphere even after the 'armistice'. The revolution of the age persisted, indeed it grew more acute and clarified itself in continually new phases. It is probably for this reason that we do not again feel the present war, like 1914, to be a radical alteration of our life, but regard it merely as another sharper clarification of our existence in a world whose character we have already sampled in principle for years. Just as a speeded-up film reveals, in a more impressive concentration, movements which otherwise would not be perceptible, so the war makes clear in a particularly vivid and unconcealed form what for years has been becoming more and more uncannily clear as the nature of the world. War isn't the first thing to bring death, to reveal the sorrows and troubles of human bodies and souls, to unleash lies, unlawfulness and violence. War isn't the first thing to make our existence so utterly insecure, to make man the impotent one, who must see his wishes and plans crossed and destroyed 'by higher authority'. But war makes all this, which has already existed without it and before it, obvious to us all, however much we would still like to overlook it.

This is the very place where the war gives us in a special way the possibility of a real Christmas. 'Farewell world' – that is the only insight from which we can grasp what it means that 'Christ is born'. But we avoid that knowledge with every possible means. It is indeed an unbearable insight. When faced with it, we want to hide our heads in the sand. It's not as bad as all that! We want to flee to some blessed isle. My life, at least, is still splendid and happy and harmonious! How often is the pastor's house and the pastor's life just such a blessed isle? And to what extent have we Germans made Christmas into just such an island, on which one can save oneself from the true reality of life for a couple of days, or at least hours. How far is all our customary festive celebration, with all the cosiness and loveliness and sweetness and gaiety with which we have adorned it, not tuned in to this 'magic', which is meant to transport us to fairyland? Christmas – just a 'holiday from myself', 'holiday from living'. So the real Christmas, as it confronts us in the journey of the shepherds to the cradle, has become days of outward and inward pleasure, for which the message of God's love might make quite a useful background.

This sort of Christmas – and we will readily concede how much it has taken this form even in the homes of pastors – has already been made difficult for us in recent years. The 'magic' has completely lost its power today; it no longer has any reality. Escapism is prohibited. It's now become clear to us that the pretty veils which used to be able to deceive us for whole hours and days are cheats and lies. The real nature of the world has been revealed. It is no longer a statement of dogmatic theology to renounce the world; it is clearly the reality in which our actual life is accomplished. So we now hear the old message with new senses and a new desire: 'Behold I bring you' – those who are in darkness and in the shadow of death – 'tidings of great joy! For to you today is born the Saviour, Jesus the Lord!' In the feast of Christmas we are directed in a new way to the very thing that stands in the centre of the Bible, to the simple reality of the gracious and merciful action which comes from God into this lost world. We are no longer concerned with elegant and gay pictures and fancies; from the reality which is so plain and from our distress, we thirst for the reality of the great divine help. Our question is whether God really has sent the One who has right and authority for complete, all-embracing, final redemption. And the Christmas message is the complete, glorious, 'Yes' of the answer to this question. It is our task, our blessed task, at Christmas to hear the message in all its simplicity and to utter it just as it stands. The world has always been full of thousands of demands, plans, summonses, exhortations with which men seek to overcome the distress of the world, which sooner or later, sadly enough, becomes evident to everyone. We do not have to demand, to plan and to exhort again, thank God, we simply have to hear and to say what has been given by God as our real, our complete, hope, without any of our doing and our working.

Of course, in this way we simply have the Christmas which the shepherds of Bethlehem had, even if we can take the whole richness of the cross, the resurrection and the ascension of Christ into our Christmas. Like the shepherds, we remain believers. Like them, we see the child in the cradle, who does not want to be distinguished from other children, and we hear the message 'as it had been told them' of this child. The night of the world is as dark to us as it was to the shepherds then. We can no more see now than they could then that the glory of the world is laid on the shoulders of this child, that all power in heaven and earth is given to him, despite all the rich and blessed experiences of all Christendom on earth; today, we can do no more than listen and believe as they did then. Our Christmas, too, does not take us out of the distress, the burdens of our life in the world; it does not take us to Paradise. We too must return again, like the shepherds, back into the old conditions, with all the pressure that chafes us. But – only let the shepherds' Christmas be given us if like them we can just hear and believe! The Saviour is there! God's hand again rests upon the world and will no longer let it go! The night is far spent, the day is already at hand! The glory of the world has already been taken from the prince of this world and laid on the shoulders of this child! In that case it can also be said of us, as of those shepherds: not only did they 'return' into all the old, bitter distress; they also 'glorified and praised God for all they had heard and seen, as it had been told them', in the midst of all their personal needs, in the midst of the night of the world, in the midst of war . . . (*Letter is incomplete*)   G.S.II pp. 570–5

The 'escapist' Christmas is rejected and the child is already one 'who does not want to be distinguished from other children'. Bonhoeffer has not yet taken the step of complete autonomy for man, 'living before God, without God'. He still gives the comforts of 'God's hand again rests upon the world and will no longer let it go'. But as the unfinished letter dies away, we can detect the questioning that will later trouble Bonhoeffer in prison, 'in the midst of the night of the world, in the midst of war . . .'

Bonhoeffer continued to write almost daily to Bethge, telling of his own experiences at the monastery at Ettal. These personal letters tell more of his inner thoughts, even when the subject matter is at times trivial:

Ettal, 1st December, Advent 1, 1940

BONHOEFFER TO BETHGE: A happy Advent! Much joy in your work and in the Advent hymns! Hans came yesterday. I've now heard all about you from him. We find that the moral of the story consists in the fact that we know too few people and the circle is too narrow. I had a long talk with Wolfhart before his illness on this very point, and he wanted to begin something like this. Now he probably won't be able to get round to it. There is therefore all the greater need for it to be begun now. It's also time we heard something about Hans. I might be able to help you in that direction before Christmas. After that I'm going away myself for quite a while. So I suggest you come here immediately after East Prussia (from the 20th onwards there will presumably be difficulties), rest for a couple of days, which you will need in any case, then visit some people with me, not just professional in the narrow sense, but with a wider horizon . . . we cannot always rely on two eyes. So I would expect you after 16th December . . . I'm then probably going to Sutz, and elsewhere. All the best. G.S.II pp. 387–8

Ettal, 5th December, 1940

BONHOEFFER TO BETHGE: In the meantime you will also have read that from the 20th onwards travelling will be more difficult. So we must decide soon. I've just heard that towards Christmas the sun no longer shines on Ettal, which lies in the valley. So perhaps we should move elsewhere. But if you are for Friedrichsbrunn, let me know in good time! I have nothing against it in itself, especially if there are not too many children up there. I'm going straight to Munich, to arrange all sorts of things. I have to report there officially. So much to talk about and discuss is piling up that it is high time we met. Justus wrote very happily about your stay there: it was a 'fruitful and lively exchange'. G.S.II p. 388

Ettal, Advent 2, 8th December, 1940

BONHOEFFER TO BETHGE: . . . Now I'm looking forward to your arrival . . . The Catholic Advent is still rather strange. I'm looking forward to Christmas with you. So keep me up to date. It's snowing like mad here. I've still not put on my snow-scarf! Together, then, as before. God bless you in all your work!

P.S. The Gürtner/Kerrl conversations seem to have gone well! G.S.II p. 389

Ettal, 10th December, 1940

BONHOEFFER TO BETHGE: . . . Of course I shall meet you in Munich. Perhaps we'll remain there for a while to settle some things straight away. Perhaps Gürtner will come with you about the same time, to meet his son. It would be very nice if you got to know him.

They were asking up here about what I did and why I came over so often. I gave them good and clear answers. One gradually gets used to everything. I'm now beginning with the section about natural life. You are right, it's dangerous material. But all the more attractive for that very reason. Goodbye. God bless you.   G.S.II p. 389

Ettal, 11th December, 1940

BONHOEFFER TO BETHGE: . . . Do you prefer to travel second-class during the day? It takes eleven hours . . . If you bring something good to read (I read Ibsen again with great excitement, *Wild Goose*, Nora, *Ghosts*, very suitable for the railway!), then perhaps it's even quite restful . . . I'm very busy with field postcards for Christmas. There are ninety of them. Today it's been snowing again without stopping. What's it like with you? There was an air-raid warning for a quarter of an hour here. Very disturbing for the inexperienced. All the best, and all power for the last days!   G.S.II pp. 389–90

Ettal, 13th December, 1940

BONHOEFFER TO BETHGE: . . . It's now been snowing here for forty-eight hours without stopping, and the snowdrifts are piling up, bigger even than last year, and extraordinary for here. I'm meeting Hans in Munich on the 16th . . .

                                   G.S.II p. 390

Bonhoeffer continued to write to Eberhard Bethge as he prepared for his first overseas visit on behalf of the Abwehr. It was a strange kind of life that he was living. While some of his students were dying at the front and others were imprisoned or suffering various persecutions, he seemed to be ideally settled, able to concentrate on his work as hardly ever before, able to visit Berlin and indulge in his music,

83

playing the quartet with his friends. Several were anxious about him, wondering why he was not in the thick of it. Even those who knew about his work with the Abwehr wondered if it were more than an excuse to keep him safe. His letters in 1941 show something of his own anxiety about this. He continued his work and justified it to Eberhard; he kept himself busy and with real excitement told of his forthcoming visit to Switzerland:

Ettal, 15th January, 1941

BONHOEFFER TO BETHGE: . . . The matter must now be pushed on as firmly as possible. There was surely no idea of action like this in December! And if the E. O. [i.e. the Ober-kirchenrat] learns that the military are already interested in the affair, it will surely be more accessible. I would definitely look into that if I were you. Above all, don't loiter over the whole thing. You owe that to Hans and the rest. I still trust your activity enough to have decided not to be disturbed for the time being. I'm getting down to work again. It's very nice to have Koch's company. Please send the dictionaries, and also the little Metoulas . . . Is Christiane really expecting us to visit them soon? I had that impression, or am I wrong? How nice that you were with Johannes yesterday . . . Read Exod. 23. 7 again. I must stop now and write to Frau Martin for her birth-day. Thanks for everything, and goodbye.   G.S.II pp. 391–2

Hotel Europäischer Hof, Munich, 17th January, 1941

BONHOEFFER TO BETHGE: This letter-head will no longer be strange to you. I've been here for a couple of days, and am going to Kloster Metten today for two days. Back again in Ettal on Monday. . . How did the Lokies business go? You've been away from Berlin for a long time. Just take care that all the necessary things happen! Hans is also going then. Good that you know O. [i.e. General Oster of the *Abwehr*], in case Hans is away. The date of my journey will be changed once again, until Hans has been. I'm just off to enquire about a visa. Yesterday evening I was with Müller again. It was satisfactory in every respect. Now I must go.

G.S.II pp. 392–3

Munich, 19th January, 1941
BONHOEFFER TO BETHGE: . . . Late yesterday evening we came by car from Metten to Munich . . . Unfortunately I couldn't reach anyone in the Ordinariate. I'm now sending a letter to Neuhäusler asking him to send you the statement immediately.

I'm not going now before the 27th or 28th, so I'll get to Berlin at the end of February. How do you like *The Last Puritan*? The Reinhold Schneider is very good.

G.S.II p. 393

Ettal, 20th January, 1941
BONHOEFFER TO BETHGE: As our correspondence will in any case be very limited in the coming weeks, it doesn't matter that we write rather more often in the last week before I go away. Today your brief letter came, with the good news about your getting the colour you wanted. [A reference to the 'red' card which allowed Bethge to undertake extra-parochial duties.] This may be a more important decision for your whole life than you can see at the moment. However many different motives there may be in things like that, it is certain that one would have to go this way if one could, on clear, objective grounds. And that is the decisive thing. I think I'm writing that because I know that I myself have a share in this decision, and any decision of a far-reaching nature calls forth a desire for justification. In this sense, then, I am quite settled and now I'm really also very glad.

John has just been and told me very happily of his visit to the Marienburger Allee, where he met you all. He was particularly enchanted with Mama. He said that he would very much have liked to come to tea with you, that he even rang twice, but could not get hold of you. He very much wanted to meet some people at your place, but he intended to come again soon. Then you must invite a few ordinary people, perhaps Böhm, Willi, Walter, Lokies, anyway people who do not just talk theologically and dogmatically (possibly Otto?). Take him to Frau Martin's as well! Justus has said that he will come here on Friday. That will be very good, before my journey.

In my work, I've now come up against the question of euthanasia. The more I come to write, the more I am attracted by the material. I find Catholic ethics in many respects most instructive, and more practical than ours. So far it's always been chalked up to them as 'casuistry'; today one is thankful for a great deal – and precisely for my present theme. I'm already looking forward very much to the conversations of the next few weeks, and I shall perhaps be able to retail some of them to you when I come to Berlin. However, the business will be a long one. Meanwhile I had to write a short article for Weckermann, on Exodus 15. 26, for a book in which W. Kramp, Vogel, etc., are also involved.

At the moment it's thawing. So I can safely stay in my room and work. You really had the best weeks. That splendid time is still in my memory every day, and as it is now Philistine to want to have it always as good as that, I'm glad it was as it was.

Now goodbye. I think every day of all the brothers in the communities.   G.S.II pp. 393–5

Ettal, 25th January, 1941

BONHOEFFER TO BETHGE: I'm not leaving until 3rd February. Stay in Berlin, if you can, at the beginning and in the middle of March. I can also arrange things to a certain extent to suit you. The reporting business will probably be settled by then. – I spoke for quite a while with Justus about Catholic affairs . . . He will tell you. Nothing new. I would like to get a bit further in March . . . – I'm glad you're interested in the Santayana. No sensational problem, but very wise and good. We must talk about it some time. I've sometimes felt that *Oliver* touches me quite deeply. Can you understand? Yesterday I was with Justus at the opera: Beethoven's *Creatures of Prometheus* as a pantomime. I was not very impressed. The Schiller film, which I saw recently, was very bad; pompous, wordy, unauthentic, unhistorical, badly acted. Kitsch! So beware! I thought of Schiller like that when I was in the fourth form . . .

G.S.II p. 395

Ettal, 27th January, 1941

BONHOEFFER TO BETHGE: I hope to see you in Berlin at the beginning of March. Then perhaps we shall be able to play the *Art of Fugue* again! G.S.II p. 396

Munich, 31st January, 1941

BONHOEFFER TO BETHGE: Once again I'm taking advantage of a stay in Munich to write a word to you. Meanwhile you will have heard of me via Koch . . . Gürtner's death was a blow to us, particularly as the children were here. They've been exceptionally brave. I'm glad that we were with him when we were. I hope that freezing walk didn't affect him, with his influenza. Of course it's now completely uncertain what will happen about the conversations with Kerrl. Perhaps Hans can take the matter in hand? I hope that I shall still be able to see him here. – My visa still hasn't arrived. The delay is a disturbing one. The day before yesterday the sergeant of the guard visited me and told me that my order to report has now been transferred to Munich, after its suspension had already been promised to me from elsewhere. I went in today, and they will give me an answer on Monday. Evidently the two things went along side by side. I'm reading Schneider with great delight. It's marvellous to have it. I would very much like to give it to you . . . I doubt whether the Schneider will be available for long. It's being bought up very quickly. Yesterday I was at Kalckreuth's with a number of nice people. You would have liked it, too. I talked especially to Franz König's brother-in-law, who has been through a great deal. I also breakfasted with him today.

Now something quite different. There are sometimes weeks during which I read the Bible very little. Something stops me. Then one day I come back to it again, and everything is so much stronger, and one can't get away from it. I don't have a very good conscience about it; but then I ask myself whether perhaps this human weakness is not also part of the thing too, and comes from the word of God. Or do you think – I really mean it – one ought to force oneself? Or isn't that always very good? We must talk about it again. How's the clavichord? Don't forget Aunt Ruth's birthday. Or mine! All the best!

G.S.II pp. 396–7

Ettal, 1st February, 1941

BONHOEFFER TO BETHGE: This time I must also write you a birthday letter . . . What splendid days we've had on my birthday, in Finkenwalde, Schlönwitz and Sigurdshof! In recent years I've done better than I deserve in this respect. I've always had a group of brothers around to support me, which gave a special spiritual stamp to the day . . .

You've also patiently endured the tests of such a friendship, particularly through my forcefulness (which I myself abhor, and which fortunately you keep on reminding me about quite openly), and you've not allowed yourself to be embittered by it . . .
G.S.II p. 397

Ettal, 4th February, 1941

BONHOEFFER TO BETHGE: The day is over, and just before I go to sleep I want to talk for a little while with you in this way, as we had to content ourselves with just a couple of minutes on the telephone. But it was splendid to be able at least to exchange a word with you. It made one's memories of other birthdays particularly vivid again, and also made one aware that a day like this is really insignificant and unimportant without that morning chorale at my door, which you arranged for me over the years, and without morning and evening prayers together, with personal intercessions. All other, all external signs of love must come into this light, or they lose their splendour. Nor is it very easy to make this background by oneself alone, especially if one is used to others. I miss Finkenwalde, Schlönwitz and Sigurdshof more and more. *Life Together* was really my swan-song. Johannes was very nice and touching, and gave me a surprise by coming over to congratulate me with two cakes, a schnapps and a wonderful azalea. My parents wrote birthday letters which I enjoyed very much, and sent me splendid things with much love. You wrote me a most companionly letter, and I'm particularly grateful for that. When things of that sort are said occasionally one is so grateful, and it does one good, especially when one can be as certain as one can be with you that every word is meant just as it has been written. At the moment, our letters are remarkably the same in content. There is no coincidence about this; it confirms that our letters reflect things as they are. Among other things, you wish me good, exciting friends. A man can indeed wish that for himself, and it's a great gift today. Yet the human heart is fashioned in such a way that it doesn't seek the plural, but just the singular, and it rests on that. The demands, the limitations and the riches of a true human relationship are that it touches on the realm of individuality and at the same time essentially depends on faithfulness. There can be individual relationships without faithfulness and there can be faithfulness without individual relationships. Both can be found in the plural. But together (which is rare enough!) they look for the singular, and happy is he who has 'succeeded in this great venture'.

That was an attractive book you sent me. I've already begun to read it with interest. I am indebted to you for Heinrich Schütz, and with him a whole rich world. I would love to accompany you in 'Hasten, O God, to deliver me', which I hummed to myself again with the help of the musical supplement. And I don't think it was a coincidence that it was you who introduced me to Schütz. I, at any rate, can see an essential connection there.

How far have you got with *Oliver*? The senselessness of his life indeed consists in his supporting every possible cause without being convinced of the inner significance of this support, with the result that he isn't free for the real, completely personal, offering of his life. He knows, is aware of, can do, wills, all that is good and beautiful and true, but it is all lifeless, and therefore superfluous. As far as men and God are concerned he never risks everything and so in the end becomes a solitary, indeed a ridiculous, figure. With its austerity, it's a book which lingers on in one's memory. Whether it gets one any further is another question; we must talk about it again another time.

It was Gürtner's funeral yesterday. Meiser preached. (The Catholics had refused! Great consternation here at the monastery. The abbot and Johannes went to the burial at our request and because of their own convictions. But please don't tell those who weren't invited, I mean about the refusal. Afterwards the abbot went to Faulhaber, who seems to have grown very old! Unfortunately!) I'm glad that you were able to meet Gürtner here.

. . . I still don't have the visa. It must come soon now. Still, we shall be able to hear from each other a bit longer. I'm looking forward to 10th March, etc. So I'll stop now for today. It's late, and I'm tired. Once again, thanks for everything.   G.S.II pp. 398–400

Ettal, 8th February, 1941

BONHOEFFER TO BETHGE: . . . I was very interested in the musical articles. Shall we buy a viola da gamba? I would be very much in favour. Practise the *Müllerlied Variations* too; I would very much like to play them with you. I enjoyed reading the Schütz-Bach book; I found the individual details good and convincing, although some things are still not very clear to me. The borderline between the portrayal of the spiritual content of, say, tears (Peter) and a realistic rendering, a translation of the physical element into music, is still somewhat obscure; I understand the essential difference, but I don't know whether it can be carried out in practice.

N.[1] was suddenly taken ill in Munich on Wednesday, and was taken to hospital. The diagnosis is still uncertain (perhaps he brought the illness back from the mission field) and he may perhaps have to have special treatment. I'm very sorry. But of course every conceivable thing is being done. How's Wolfgang? What's up with Gabriel? . . . My journey will be postponed still longer because of technical difficulties. The answer was negative at first. Now they're trying again. So Berlin and our meeting is all off before the middle of March . . . My reporting has been settled for the time being while I'm here at Munich. It's thawing again here . . .   G.S.II pp. 400–1

---

[1] Prelate Neuhäusler. The information is in code: hospital=prison; mission field=the hostile attitude to Rome in the Western world; special treatment=concentration camp.

Ettal, 10th February, 1941

BONHOEFFER TO BETHGE: . . . Today I'm going to Munich for the day with Christel. I want to have another word with the consul before he goes. Reporting was transferred from Köslin to Munich and cancelled there, so Köslin are no longer concerned. It's been spring here for two days. Wonderful, but the end of skiing . . .

I'm now on the question of marriage (the right of free choice of spouse, marriage laws according to racial or confessional viewpoints, Rome, Nuremberg, sterilization, contraception, etc.). Catholic morals are in fact almost intolerably legalistic about all these things. I had a long conversation with the abbot and Johannes about them. They thought that the attitude of the Church towards contraception was the chief reason why most men no longer come to confession. The practice of confession on this point seems to me to be very dangerous. There is of course no absolution without repentance, but what sort of a repentance is it which is proved false again every three days? That makes for hypocrisy. In fact, the action is simply not recognized as sinful, and in that case nothing makes sense. I think that one must allow a great deal of freedom here. What do you think? – I find your thoughts about *Oliver* good. *Simplicissimus?* Perhaps, I'm still not sure. Don't get involved in locums pure and simple in East Prussia. Keep off them as a matter of principle. There's no point in spoiling your work for them. One should be stricter and more determined than I was then, and than you usually are. It's necessary for one's work.
G.S.II pp. 401–2

Ettal, 14th February, 1941

BONHOEFFER TO BETHGE: . . . You'll also be needing and keeping a firm time for prayer in the morning, now that your life is so unsettled. It also clarifies what one is to do and say during the day, and one becomes 'independent' in daily decisions . . . My time of waiting here has not been wasted; I've been able to write again very well during the last few days. But of course I would be very glad to have the journey behind me. Schmidhuber is going there today and is trying to settle the thing in person. Then I'll get the news by telegram. I only hope that you will be free for a while then. I can easily arrange things to suit you. But you must be in Berlin again. I'm particularly looking forward to music with you . . . I think, though, that you will be the one who learns the viola da gamba! I'm too old for it. It's no longer worth it! . . . Take care, too, that such superfluous notebooks don't get printed again. Have you read *Proclamation and Scholarship?* Very interesting. Asmussen is taken up in it, which is very good. Are you going to join the Society for Protestant Theology? Anyway, keep this to yourself – I haven't joined yet, but I shall have to. If we don't, who else will? Then one has the books sent free. The poems by Adolf Schlatter about John the Baptist and so on which are now appearing are quite astonishing. So far I've been reading them with great pleasure.

Wonderful weather today. Frost, sun, but no snow. Goodbye, greetings to all the people I know: Koschorke, Jänicke, Kramp, . . . Beckmann, etc. God bless you.   G.S.II pp. 402–3

Ettal, 15th February, 1941

BONHOEFFER TO BETHGE: It was a wonderful surprise to get you today at my parents' . . . Did I disturb Mama at work this evening? That would have been a pity. My chief work period now is really in the afternoon. There's a great deal of quiet, and little interruption. – Otherwise things have been going very well over the past few days. I've now finished with the difficult questions of sterilization and contraception. Now it's a matter of natural law on work, freedom, thought. Sometimes

I'm afraid and worried that the flesh is playing a considerable part alongside the spirit.

Now goodbye. Don't bother about the clavichord. If the tone isn't so good, it doesn't matter all that much. If a bomb falls on it, it's finished anyway; if one doesn't, then we can mend it later. Perhaps Neupert can also do something through his firm in Berlin. All best wishes for the journey. God be with you.

On the reverse of this card there is a saying of Angelus Silesius:

Man, give your heart to God, and he will bestow;
See what a good exchange; you rise, he stoops.

Pencilled note:

I'm really surprised at this saying. Apart from all the dogmatic questions it raises, it's never like this in practice, but always the other way round. If God's heart is not opened to me in his word, then I simply cannot raise my heart to him. Or do you find that it is right the other way round, too?

G.S.II pp. 403–4

Ettal, 17th February, 1941
BONHOEFFER TO BETHGE: . . . Wurm wrote here today at length, and very personally and nicely, about my recent letter. I'm sending you the letter as soon as I've shown it to Johannes. What sort of decisions may the next few weeks bring? Goodbye. Thanks again for everything. Shall I send you the brothers' birthday letter?
G.S.II p. 404

Ettal, 19th February, 1941
BONHOEFFER TO BETHGE: It now looks as though I shall be able to travel, presumably leaving Munich on the 23rd or 24th, for about four weeks. I'm going to Munich on the 21st, and will stay as usual at the Europäischer Hof.

I will give Erwin, and, if possible, Lang, your greetings.

Yesterday M. told me that Aunt H. has inoperable cancer of the liver and that the doctor gives her four to six months to live. That will affect M. a great deal. It makes you think. What would I do, if I knew that it would be all over in four to six months' time? That's going through my head. I think I should still try to teach theology as I used to and to preach as much as possible.

Wurm also sent me his lecture and asked for an opinion. I must also do that before I go. If it interrupts my work considerably, I hope that I shall also benefit from it. Now goodbye . . .

It will now be the end of March before we see each other. Ten weeks. It often seems to be so senseless. The *Müllerlied Variations* will sound all the better, though . . .

G.S.II pp. 404–5

Ettal, 22nd February, 1941

BONHOEFFER TO BETHGE: Today I've made the necessary arrangements. I'm going the day after tomorrow. I'll hardly be able to write to you after that . . . So don't be surprised . . . Good that you were able to discuss you-know-what with N.N. I think that morally nothing can really be said against suicide; it is a sin of unbelief, but that is no moral disqualification. I don't think I've yet told you that at Gürtner's funeral the Regensburg cathedral choir, to which he himself used to belong, sang, first 'Lord let thine angels carry him to Abraham's bosom', then 'O sacred head'. The 'Though now by insult tortured, all glory be to thee' was especially moving. At the end there was a sentence I didn't know from Job 19. The family had asked for the hymns. It was the best part of the whole ceremony. In any case, I'm always particularly affected by funerals. The question of what remains in the face of death cannot be avoided on such occasions. That's the time when penitence about uselessness and perverseness especially takes hold of one, and along with it the hope of a life that will stand in the face of death. But rises are always followed by a fall, and a tremendous up and down. Will it ever be otherwise?

I saw the Bismarck film yesterday. Not bad. Amusingly enough, Bismarck reminded me of Lasbeck. I'm still writing to Frau von Kleist. – The chalices will be consecrated when I leave Ettal. There was general admiration of them, and they were thought to be a wedding present, and great revelations were expected from me. Unfortunately I had to disappoint them . . . I shall be in Munich again on 24th March. Goodbye. I'll write to you again briefly before I go. God bless you.

G.S.II pp. 405–6

Munich, 23rd February, 1941

BONHOEFFER TO BETHGE: I'm sitting in the Schotzenhamel and waiting for my supper. As minutes are valuable now, I want to write a brief note to you. The question I'm most concerned about is, How well off are you in fact for marks? Are you all right? Otherwise I can send you something again, or bring it when I get back. – My post is going to the Marienburger from now on – would you please open it? Do you think the idea about Friedrichsbrunn and the possible visit together is a good one? (*The rest of this letter is lost.*)

G.S.II p. 406

3. The Influence of Geneva

Bonhoeffer spent one month in Switzerland, 24th February–24th March, 1941. There had been delays on the German side, but it was not easy for a German to enter Switzerland without a guarantee. Bonhoeffer named Karl Barth as his guarantor, but Barth tells how dubious he was. He could not understand how a man like Bonhoeffer could leave Germany with valid papers, unless he had gone over to the other side! It was not until the return journey that Bonhoeffer was able to visit Barth and explain everything.

His four weeks in Switzerland were spent mostly in Zürich and Geneva. He was anxious to see Erwin Sutz who had enabled him to maintain contacts with the Leibholz family in Oxford. He also saw Siegmund-Schultze. But his main objective was Geneva. Most of the World Council of Churches staff were too busy to give him much time, because they were concerned with relief work among prisoners of war. But the exception was Visser 't Hooft, who gave him all the time he wanted. It is from a letter written by him to George Bell, the Bishop of Chichester, that we have the clearest picture of Bonhoeffer during this first visit to Geneva. The letter is quoted in Eberhard Bethge's biography, and again here for convenience:

19th March, 1941

VISSER 'T HOOFT TO CHICHESTER: Bonhoeffer was a week with us and spent most of his time extracting ecumenical information from persons and documents. It is touching to see how hungry people like him are for news about their brothers in other countries, and it is good to know that he can take back so much which will encourage his friends at home.

On the other hand, we learned a lot from him. The picture which he gave is pretty black in respect to the exterior circumstances for the community which he represents [i.e. the Confessing Church]. The pressure is greater than ever. But fortunately he could also tell of many signs that their fundamental position has not changed at all and that they are as eager as ever for fellowship. Many of them have really the same reaction to all that has happened and is happening as you or as I have. And this is remarkable after such a long period of isolation. I hope to send soon through Bill some fuller notes on all that we learned through him about the situation.

Visser 't Hooft recognized that Bonhoeffer had the clearest picture of the political dilemma and reports it equally clearly:

Inside the Confessing Church there is a certain difference of conviction with regard to the stand which the Church should take. There is, on the one hand, a group which believes that the Church should stick to what is called 'the inner line', and concentrate exclusively on the building up of its own spiritual life. This tendency is often combined with a strongly apocalyptic note. There is, on the other hand, a group which believes that the Church has also a prophetic and ethical function in relation to the world and that it must prepare for the moment when it can again fulfil that function.

With regard to the attitude to the war, it is generally recognized among believing Christians that a victory of their government will have the most fateful consequences for the Church in their own country as well as in other countries. On the other hand, they consider that a defeat of their country would probably mean its end as a nation. Thus many have come to believe that whatever the outcome of it all will be, it will be an evil thing for them. One hears, however, also voices which say that after all the suffering which their country has brought upon others they almost hope for an opportunity to pay the price by suffering themselves.

Bonhoeffer returned to Germany on 24th March, 1941, but assured his Geneva friends that he would be back soon. His confidence in the ecumenical movement seems to have been restored, thanks to Visser 't Hooft.

A few days after his return, Bonhoeffer received a communication from the office controlling publications of writings by undesirable authors. He considered the matter carefully and sent the following reply:

BONHOEFFER TO THE REICH DEPARTMENT FOR WRITING: On 27th March, 1941, I received by registered letter from the Reich Department for Writing a notice to pay a fine of 30 R.M., and at the same time I was barred from all activity as a writer. I have paid the fine, without being able to acknowledge its justification. I appeal both against the fine and against the prohibition on the following grounds:

1. The official notification No. 88, para. 2, runs: 'Anyone who publishes purely academic works as a scholar, in his own special field, does not fall under the jurisdiction of the Reich Department for Writing.' A statement by the Reich Minister for the Interior on 4.11.34 runs: 'Officials, scholars, ministers, doctors and lawyers do not fall under the jurisdiction of the Reich Department for Writing if they do scholarly work within their professional sphere.' All my publications have been summaries of the results of my academic research, in dogmatics, ethics and exegesis. They therefore do not fall within the jurisdiction of the Reich Department for Writing and I am not therefore obliged to report to that department. Besides, it is almost incomprehensible that I should have been

notified as late as 1941 that I should have reported a work published in 1937.

2. I wish to make the following observations about the details of the works listed in your communication: The book *The Cost of Discipleship* (1937) has been universally recognized in theological circles as a purely academic work (see the discussion in *Theologische Literaturzeitung*, etc.). *Life Together* (1938) appeared in the academic series *Theologische Existenz* and is addressed to theologians. *The Prayerbook of the Bible: Introduction to the Psalms* (1940) covers only 16 pages and therefore comes under para. 3 of the official notification No. 88 about writings 'on a small scale', which need not be reported. The writing contains the results of academic work. The collection *Helps to Preaching* gives academic expositions of texts for preachers, which the laity would not be able to use. So not a single one of my publications calls for the fine that has been imposed.

3. The list of my writings which was sent when the fine was imposed is so inaccurate that I must assume that the writings themselves were not consulted. I have never written a book entitled *Year Together*; the proper title is *Life Together*. The title *Prayerbook of the Bible* is omitted from *Introduction to the Psalms*. No collection entitled *Sermon Letters* exists; I co-operated in the work *Helps to Preaching*, which was published not by the G. Müller Verlag but by the E. Müller Verlag.

4. I cannot acknowledge the justification of the prohibition against publishing further books, nor of the prohibition which I have received against speaking in public. When I received the latter, I protested against the general charges made against me, giving detailed reasons in writing. So far the reasons I gave have neither been acknowledged nor rejected. Moreover, it must be clear to everyone who knows my academic publica-

tions that these are controversies carried on purely within theology, which cannot have anything in the least to do with the reasons for the prohibition against speaking which has been imposed upon me.

During a stay in East Prussia in the summer of 1940, I was invited in Königsberg, by one of the pastors there, to take a Bible study and a lecture for a small gathering of students outside Königsberg. I expressed my readiness to do this, and on 13.7.40 I met about six people, comprising three students and three members of the congregation, in Blöstau. I took a Bible study on the story of the rich young ruler. The next morning I took the service. I intended to lecture in the afternoon on 'the problem of death'. While I was sitting with the students, having an informal conversation after the service, a number of officials of the Secret Police came, broke up the meeting, and interrogated those present. Our attention was drawn to a decree of 26th April, 1940, according to which the prohibition of Confessional youth organizations can also be extended to similar adult organizations. None of us could have known about this decree, which was never published. The officials of the Secret Police expressed their surprise at the small number of those present, and one said that they would not have come had they known. I was told personally that no further inconveniences would hinder me as a result of this occasion as I was involved in the organization only by chance, as a visitor. No individual charges were made against me. I am personally convinced that the prohibition was not the result of any particular statements but of the fact that during my stay in East Prussia I preached in very well attended churches in a number of places.   G.S.II pp. 369–71

He received a bureaucratic reply, acknowledging that certain theologians who occupied recognized positions in the state colleges were exempt, but that Bonhoeffer could not be recognized as an 'academic' in this sense.

A few snatches from letters over the next few months show something of his uneasy attachment to his work. He was neither one thing nor another. From Friedrichsbrunn, 22nd April:

BONHOEFFER TO HIS PARENTS: It was splendid to have a couple of peaceful days with you, but now I am back at work. In between writing and studying, I have been hacking away at a piece of wood. I am going to make it into a cross for my wall.

From Klein-Krössin, end of June:

BONHOEFFER TO HIS PARENTS: I've been enjoying the quietness of country life again for a couple of days. I'm working well and taking my exercise in the garden.

From Klein-Krössin, 5th July:

BONHOEFFER TO HIS PARENTS: I wanted to go to Berlin towards the end of next week to spend a couple of days there before I have to go to Munich. No further news of the sons and grandsons of the families there . . . Of course the news from the war is being followed with the greatest interest, and some people are already beginning to get impatient that it isn't over yet. That is of course very childish. From all they hear, the people here seem to think that the resistance is particularly tough and that disturbs them!   G.S.II p. 407

Perhaps more telling than his own letters is one from Frau von Kleist, about him. It was written to Bethge and dated 24th August, 1941:

FRAU VON KLEIST TO BETHGE: . . . Dietrich has written such a splendid and appropriate letter to the brethren. It's very, very important that he continues to do that . . . Perhaps that's

D.'s only job now. I'm sometimes rather worried about him, as it can't be good for him to be so unoccupied. You have the advantage of being tied up with things . . . I now seem to be living almost in a dreamworld. The size of this latest reality is too big to grasp. One lives between heaven and earth. And one hears of new casualties every day. Each news bulletin opens the wounds afresh, and again confronts one with the questions which Dietrich sketches out in the letter I've mentioned: war, death, the future. I've become aware of belonging to these frightful events in a new way. I understand that when my son heard the news of Constantine's retreat, on the orders of my nephew Tresckow, he telegraphed Tresckow that he didn't agree . . . I don't know whether you can understand what I feel. Dietrich would probably reject this thought outright. Probably it has grown in me as a result of the countless letters of sympathy from friends and officers of our boys and above all as a result of their death, with which I have had to struggle. When I hear how bravely our children died, I tell myself that it was not only spiritual strength that enabled them to do so, but also an instinct that compelled them to the whole venture. I know one cannot derive a law from that, that things must be as they seem to me to be at present. In your case I'm counting on your knowledge of my ways for you not to overestimate my words.

Something in me is still quite shattered. When our news bulletins speak of the 'inconceivable casualties' which we are inflicting on the enemy, it's like a dagger in my soul.

We still have no news of Constantine. On 1st August we telegraphed to him about the death and burial of Hans Friedrich. On the 7th, the same about Jürgen Christoph. The retreat took place in the meantime. Fabian wrote on the 17th, my son's telegram. The protest (the one to the army group also took five days) had come too late. Constantine was already retreating. Since then we've been waiting daily for a sign of life from him. One's whole life is almost entirely made up of waiting. I almost imagine that he did not want to go on without looking for the graves of his brothers. In that case, it could still be a long time before he comes . . .　　G. S. II pp. 408-9

Two days later she wrote again to Bethge:

FRAU VON KLEIST TO BETHGE: I've had a bad conscience over my doubts about your way. How can I know what is binding on you? Excuse me for prematurely expressing an opinion which really wasn't an opinion, but a sensation. I've already had my doubts about it again. Oh, 'let each one be sure of his opinion'. It's probably the particular temptation of our time that we have to feel our way from one day to another and from one consideration to another.

Constantine's just arrived . . . For three days on the way to Rostock, and then we hope he'll be back again for rather longer. It's very touching to see him. Half a day after he got out, while he was still with the 'baggage', his battery came under heavy fire with considerable casualties, when it had hardly been threatened at all before. He lost his lieutenant, with whom he had been all the time. So God really meant to preserve him. 'I was just very unfortunate not to be there', he said. They couldn't discover who had ordered the recall. 'Not my father', he said. But when he had the news that Jurgen Christoph had also been killed, he did not refuse. 'First I must see how things are at home.' They were particularly good in letting him go and gave him a special commendation to Rostock. It strikes me that the soldiers at the front are made of different stuff from those at home. More reliable, more harmless, more limited.

Bonhoeffer was preparing for his second visit to Switzerland and this filled his letters at that time. It almost seemed as though he gave too little concern to the burning problems of the war. Certainly his letters are in marked contrast to those of Frau von Kleist. He wrote to Eberhard Bethge from Munich on 26th August, 1941:

Munich, 26th August, 1941

BONHOEFFER TO BETHGE: It will probably turn out that I leave here on your birthday . . . I shall be thinking of so many splendid journeys together, especially 1936 and 1939, of horizons we enlarged together, which are connected with those journeys, of hopes and tasks for Europe, of the task of the Church in the future – and I shall do so in the hope that you and I and many, many others who are of one mind will all be able to work together one day for the future. What else could I wish you in this new year but that you live and work in whatever way befalls you and that you also make those personal plans for your future which at present are still forbidden us? And I see how these wishes for you are like my own wishes. One cannot imagine how the year will go. But I'm very confident.

Perhaps we sometimes run the risk of forgetting in all these hopes the one who alone can bring them to pass and who also can take a quite different way. Perhaps we have prayed too little recently. In that case, may God forgive us and lead us back into prayer. I had a good long conversation with M. (who sends you hearty greetings) about the question of evangelical monasteries and orders. Johannes, too, was asking after you and sent his greetings. It was a very fine reunion. After Metten I couldn't do more because of the cobbles. I'll do it on the way back. Get Reimer to give you the honey he promised me and keep it all for yourself . . . Hans said to me that he would discuss your case with a Herr Olbricht in case the problems of January of this year and April of last are repeated. But that's only if it gets acute again. I hope not. I'll write again before the journey. Have a good birthday! I wish I was there. Greetings to your mother. God bless you in the new year. G.S.II pp. 411–12

Two days later, he wrote in festive mood for Eberhard's birthday:

Munich, *28th August, 1941*

BONHOEFFER TO BETHGE: The eve of your birthday gives me another quiet opportunity of writing to you once again before I go off. I almost went to the cinema in your honour but, as usual, I prefer a peaceful conversation with you to the doubtful pleasure of the film (though *The Holm Murder* sounds very promising!). If you've had as good weather as we have here, you'll now be celebrating your birthday somewhere on the Havel. I'm very glad. I've been thinking of you a good deal today. In the morning I was delighted with the splendid reading. It turns one's attention to the future of the Church, to what Christ has done for us, and finally to our ministry. If we are to be 'shepherds' of the community, as Christ was, that means much more than saying that we are to be preachers. All the descriptions of ministry in the NT (*apostolos, prophetes, didaskalos, poimēn*) are indeed original designations of the offices of Christ; they were used by Christ himself. The ministry, too, presupposes an equality of form with Christ. That is the high value of the ministry. How good to be reminded of that again. Men need shepherds, Christ was the shepherd, and through him and like him we should be shepherds of men. I myself am thankful to have rediscovered this saying. If only the prohibition which still prevents us from exercising this ministry freely were soon to be lifted – if only our thoughts could again be devoted undividedly to this task. Incidentally, the reading for the 27th was also splendid. So I hope that you will be satisfied in your reading throughout the year.

In the morning I had to make some more preparations for my journey. At noon I had a festive meal in your honour. I've also become conscious, in this lamentable business of eating in restaurants, which have also gone down enormously here, how dreadfully off you are in Berlin. Now you must exploit Reimer systematically. You can promise him coffee, perhaps even take him some . . . He likes it very much . . . How tedious good eating will be in Switzerland, all by myself. Perels rang up today from Salzburg, only to say goodbye, and he wanted to let his uncle know some things . . . I think that you should learn some more English again. Who knows when you might need it? . . . The news about Staude disturbs me considerably. It is really quite dreadful. If you're writing to your mother, remember me to her, tell her that I'm travelling and can't write now . . . I will try not to worry if I hear of attacks on Berlin. At least be sensible! Now goodbye, dear E., I'll be back on September 25th or 26th at the latest. I'll remember you to everyone. God bless you. Practise, and find something new for the flute! Greetings to your mother!

G.S.II pp. 412–14

While he was in Geneva on this second visit, Bonhoeffer saw a book by William Paton called The Church and the New Order. *It had been published in July by the Student Christian Movement Press in London. Hugh Martin, the director of the press at that time, had sent a copy to Visser 't Hooft, who responded at once:*

12th September, 1941
VISSER 'T HOOFT TO MARTIN: Many thanks for sending Bill Paton's book. It is being eagerly read by all who are in touch with us, not least by those whom it concerns in a very special manner. I enclose a Continental reaction. Will you pass this document on to Bill with the following message:
These comments on your book have been written by me in

close collaboration with a friend who came to us and who is a good friend of George Bell. I hope you will circulate them to all who are interested and also send a copy to Pit Van Dusen. You must accept my word for it that all that we say about the next steps and the urgency of the situation is not based upon wishful thinking on our part, but on actual developments in discussion with responsible persons in the country concerned. This is also why I hope that some of these considerations will be brought before responsible people in Britain. I must ask you not to publish the document as it is, but there is no reason why its substance cannot be used in the *Christian News Letter.* In that case, however, no clue should be given as to the authorship. We should, of course, appreciate some answer to this statement, and, if possible, in the near future. Very good greetings.   G.S.I. p. 361

The friend referred to is Dietrich Bonhoeffer, although his name could not safely be mentioned in the correspondence. The 'comments' are as follows:

THE CHURCH AND THE NEW ORDER IN EUROPE

The following reflections about the problem of the post-war order in Europe represent the thinking of two Continental Christians from two nations which are on opposite sides in this war. They have read William Paton's *The Church and the New Order* with deep interest, and desire to express their admiration and gratitude for this witness rendered in a truly ecumenical spirit. They have also studied the recent issues of the *Christian News Letter* which deal with post-war problems.

1. *Some basic considerations*
The insecurity of life and the tremendous upheavals have made

Continental Christians acutely conscious of the fact that the future is in God's hands and that no human planning, however intelligent and however well-intentioned, can make men masters of their own fate. There is, therefore, in Continental Churches today a strongly apocalyptic trend. This trend may lead to an attitude of pure other-worldliness, but it may also have the more salutary effect of making us realize that the kingdom of God has its own history which does not depend upon political events, and that the life of the Church has its own God-given laws which are different from those which govern the life of the world. We are, therefore, glad that Paton emphasizes so strongly that the life of the Church does not depend upon victory in the war. But this does not mean that Continental Christians are indifferent to the problem of the post-war order. Many who had previously considered that the Church had nothing to do with such secular problems have come to see in these last years that the Church is truly the salt of the earth and that the discarding of God's commandments means death for nations as well as individuals.

There is very especially a new recognition of the implications of the New Testament faith: that Christ is the King to whom all powers are subjected. Because the world is created 'for him' (Col. I. 16), we dare not consider it as a domain which lives by itself, quite apart from God's plan. The commandments of God indicate the limits which dare not be transgressed, if Christ is to be Lord. And the Church is to remind the world of these limits. For a long time it has not exercised this ministry, but more recently it has again begun to do so, as in different countries it has taken a strong stand against the violation of God's commandments in political life.

Now the task of the Church in relation to the 'new order' is to be seen in the light of this ministry. The Church cannot and should not elaborate detailed plans of post-war reconstruction, but it should remind the nations of the abiding commandments and realities which must be taken seriously if the new order is to be a true order, and if we are to avoid another judgement of God such as this present war.

We are deeply grateful that there has grown up a community of Christians of different nations which can undertake this task as a common task. We have good reason to hope that that community will come out of this war as an even more united body than it was before the war. Those who are conscious of their membership in this fellowship are as yet a small group, but they are nevertheless not unimportant, because they are practically the only international community which remains united in spite of war and conflict.

2. Why peace aims?

We agree with Paton as to the urgency of a clear statement of peace aims. But, as far as the Continent is concerned, we would say that this is especially necessary in view of the situation in *Germany*. The occupied countries have become sufficiently aware of the true character of the National-Socialist régime and are acutely conscious of the fact that their future depends on a British victory. There is, therefore, remarkably little criticism of the British blockade in these countries. But the situation in Germany is entirely different. In that country the attitude of the considerable groups who are against the régime, but are at the same time good patriots, depends on the answer which is given to the question: How will Germany be treated if it loses the war? A positive statement of peace aims may have a very strong influence in strengthening the hands of this group. It is clear that recent events have created a psychological situation in which they have an opportunity such as they have not had since 1933. There is, therefore, reason to give very great prominence to this aspect of the whole question.

Now it is clear that the very strong emphasis on the military disarmament of Germany in recent statements (and on the radio) has an unfavourable effect on this development. The only group which can take action against the régime is the army (revolutionary action from other quarters would be suppressed by the SS). Now the opposition groups in the army are not likely to act unless they have reason to believe that there is a prospect of a more or less tolerable peace. In these circumstances statements about the future (and very especially the propaganda by radio) should at least give the opposition in Germany some basis of action.

We understand that the disarmament of Germany will have to be demanded. But it should certainly not be mentioned as the main peace aim, as is being done too often. It should rather be mentioned as part of a much wider programme, which would include the giving of a certain amount of political and economic security to a disarmed Germany, and the acceptance by all nations of a certain supra-national control of their armaments. In any case, far wider use should be made in all propaganda (especially in broadcasts to Germany) of all that is being thought out in the realm of economic reconstruction and social change. Such documents as the Malvern Report have made a deep impression in opposition circles in Germany. Why does the BBC say so little about these things?

3. *The chaos behind the war*

There is an important point which Paton has not mentioned in his description of the chaos behind the war. The deepest reason for the moral confusion in Germany, and to some extent in Europe as a whole, is not merely the opposition against Christian ethical convictions (for this by itself might have created clear fronts rather than 'chaos'), but rather the ability of National Socialism to present its injustice as true justice. The railway wagon of Compiègne is as it were the symbol of this masking of injustice. There was just enough relative justice in some of Germany's claims to make it possible for Hitler to present himself as a prophet who came to re-establish justice. This is the main source of the present moral confusion. And it should not be forgotten that, by making concessions to Hitler which had been refused to his predecessors, the statesmen of other nations became the supporters of Hitler against the opposition groups in Germany. In this way it is explicable that it has become increasingly difficult for the German nation to understand the true character of the régime, and that relatively few have remained unshaken in their own conviction that it represented Satan masquerading as an angel of light.

4. Guiding principles

We consider it very important that Paton seeks the basis of the new order, not in any particular form of government, but in certain fundamental principles concerning the life of the State and of society. For it must be said with great emphasis that in a number of European countries an immediate return to full-fledged democracy and parliamentarism would create even greater disorder than that which obtained before the era of authoritarianism. In those countries (Germany, France, Italy) where all centres of political creativeness and order have been discredited or destroyed there will for a considerable time to come be a need of strong centralized authority. Democracy can only grow in a soil which has been prepared by a long spiritual tradition. Such a tradition still exists in the smaller nations (Scandinavia, Holland, Switzerland), but not in most other nations of Europe.

But this does not mean that we must continue to accept forms of state absolutism. The minimum which must be required of every state, and which must be guaranteed *internationally* (we now know that political régimes are not merely the affair of the nation concerned!), is that the State shall be limited by *law*, that is to say that it shall recognize certain binding obligations to its citizens and to other states.

The Anglo-Saxon world summarizes the struggle against the omnipotence of the State in the word 'freedom'. And Paton gives us a charter of human 'rights and liberties' which are to provide the norm of action by the State. But these expressions must, as Paton indicates, 'be translated into terms which relate them more closely to the life of other peoples'. For freedom is too negative a word to be used in a situation where *all* order has been destroyed. And liberties are not enough when men seek first of all for some minimum security. These words remind too much of the old liberalism which because of its failures is itself largely responsible for the development towards State absolutism.

This is partly a quarrel of words, about the realities which lie behind such expressions as 'civilian religious liberties', 'freedom of speech' or 'equality of all before the law', which must certainly be safeguarded in the new order. But it is also much more than a matter of words. For the whole orientation of the post-war states will depend on this ideological question. Now we believe that the conception of order limited by law and responsibility, an order which is not an aim in itself, but which recognizes commandments which transcend the State, has more spiritual substance and solidity than the emphasis on the rights of individual men.

Thus it is certainly true – as Paton indicates – that in a country like Germany it will be impossible to introduce all the various forms of democratic liberties. But it will be possible, as in other countries, to do away with all forms of National-Socialist terrorism, to make law once more the impartial arbiter, not only between citizens, but also between citizens and the State, and to give full freedom to the Church. If then safeguards are formulated concerning the régimes of countries which have been totalitarian (will Russia be included among these?), they should be couched, not so much in terms of individual rights, but in terms of norms which the State must recognize in all its actions.

5. *The ideal and the next steps*

We agree whole-heartedly with the conception of international order which is given in Paton's chapter on 'The Ideal and the Next Steps'. We are especially glad that he makes it clear that this order cannot be a mere restoration of the pre-war political and economic system. For it has become very clear on the Continent (and is understood by many who did not understand this a few years ago) that there must come drastic changes in these two domains. In the political domain there must be effective limitation of national sovereignty. In the economic domain there must be limitation of economic individualism, in other words, planning for economic security of the masses.

But, as Paton says, 'the ultimate settlement is bound to be influenced profoundly by the nature of the temporary measures which are taken in the interim period, and upon the proper shaping of those measures the future may depend'. Now we do not believe that Paton's book throws yet sufficient light on this problem. And we do not believe that the solution of this problem which is presented in the *Christian News Letter* of August 20th (Dr Oldham's summary of a P.E.P. report, which he considers to be 'entirely right' in its approach to the problem) is adequate.

We do not deny that Great Britain has the right to demand safeguards against a return of National Socialism in one form or another, and that it may therefore have to take far-reaching military measures against Germany. But we feel that for the sake of the future these unavoidable measures must be counter-balanced by a positive policy. Now it is recognized in England and America that this time there must not be a repetition of the economic clauses of the Versailles treaty, and that is indeed an important insight. But that is not enough. There remains the question as to how Germany may find its way back to a system of government which is acceptable to the Germans and also be an orderly member of the family of nations. Now this question is not answered by the total occupation of Germany (though such occupation may prove necessary). On the contrary. The total disarmament and the occupation of Germany will make it exceptionally difficult, if not impossible, to create a new German government. Would a government which accepted such conditions not be regarded as a mere Quisling affair? Would not those groups which are definitely anti-Nazi feel that even Hitler was better than this complete collapse of German integrity? Would this not lead to an even wilder form of German nationalism?

The question must then be faced whether it is possible to offer such terms of peace to Germany that a new government composed of non-Nazi German leaders who are ready for international collaboration may not be discredited from the outside in the eyes of their own people. Or to put it the other way round: the question must be faced whether a German government which makes a complete break with Hitler and all he stands for can hope to get such terms of peace that it has some chance to survive. If such a government were formed, if it made a genuine peace offer (evacuation of *all* occupied territories, ousting of all Nazi leaders, willingness to disarm), and if then this offer were rejected, there would be danger that Germans of all sections and groups would be thrown into the nationalist opposition, and that for a very long time to come no German government worthy of that name could be formed.

It is clear that the answering of this question is a matter of urgency, since the attitude of opposition groups in Germany depends upon the answer given. Realism demands that the world should be safeguarded against a return of National Socialism, but realism demands also that we should safeguard the world against a repetition of the psychological process which has taken place in Germany between 1918 and 1933. We believe that it is possible to find men in Germany who have shown by their attitude during these last years that they are not infected with National-Socialist ideas, and who can be counted upon as loyal collaborators in a European community of nations. And we believe that they should be given a chance for the sake, not only of Germany, but of Europe as a whole.

6. *The Russian problem*
It is understandable that in the present situation the problem of the relation of Russia to the future international order is not being treated as thoroughly as the problem of Germany. There is so much uncertainty as to the forces which are at work in Russia today, and as to the effect which the war will have upon them, that it is almost impossible to visualize just what its place will be. But as Christians we dare not let ourselves be carried away by momentary reactions. Even though we may consider the British-Russian alliance a justifiable and unavoidable political decision, we must not minimize the danger which Russia still represents for all that we hold dear. Unless the war calls forth very fundamental changes in the structure of the Russian state, Bolshevism may well become a tremendous menace to all countries which have been betting on the wrong horse and which will find their Fascist systems discredited by a German defeat. This is then another very strong confirmation

of the necessity for authoritarian, though non-Fascist, régimes in the post-war era, and also of the necessity of strengthening the hands of those non-Nazi elements in Germany which would be able to form a new government in that country. There is, furthermore, the very difficult question as to whether the Baltic States, the Bukovina, Karelia, Bessarabia, shall go back to a Russia which recognizes civil and religious liberties just as little as do the Nazis.   G.S.I pp. 362–71

The other author of that paper, Visser 't Hooft, wrote many years later, recalling the incident and their work together, that he saw it as part of Bonhoeffer's incredible move towards resistance. It was in this way that the theologian abandoned the quiet of his study and came out into the tempest of living.

PART TWO

The Double Agent

1941 *16th October* – First mass deportation of Jews from Berlin.
'Operation 7' in close collaboration with Dohnanyi.
7th December – Pearl Harbor.
11th December – Declaration of war by USA.

1942 *5th April* – Easter in Klein-Krössin.
10th–18th April – Journey to Norway and Sweden with Helmuth von Moltke.
May – Third journey to Switzerland – preparations for 'Operation 7'.
30th May–2nd June – Flight to Stockholm to meet Bishop Bell.
30th June–30th July – Bishop Bell approaches British and American political leaders, with no result.
5th September – Small Jewish group ('Operation 7') arrives in Switzerland.
September – Bonhoeffer's application for permit to travel in the Balkans and Switzerland refused.
8th November – Allied landing in North Africa.
24th November – Bonhoeffer's private visit to Pätzig to discuss with Frau von Wedemeyer his forthcoming engagement to her daughter.

1943 *14th January* – Declaration from Casablanca of 'unconditional surrender' as only acceptable terms for Germany.
17th January – Bonhoeffer's engagement to Maria von Wedemeyer.
March– Several attempts to assassinate Hitler.
31st March – Celebration of Bonhoeffer's father's 75th birthday.

1. 'Operation 7'

In the nature of things there are few documents about Bonhoeffer's part in the conspiracy to overthrow Hitler. We know that he was appointed to the Abwehr, a kind of intelligence corps of the armed forces, where the conspiracy under Admiral Canaris had its centre. This, however, was usual among pastors of the Confessing Church, who would not legalize themselves as incumbents under the Nazi-dominated State Church. These appointments enabled these pastors to be registered for extra-parochial service and thus evade military service. Bonhoeffer denied that he was evading military service and argued that he was putting his ecumenical contacts at the service of the State. He was appointed to the Abwehr at the end of October 1940. After that he continued his work with former Finkenwalde students. His journeys to Switzerland appeared harmless enough. For the rest he continued his valuable theological work and kept up regular correspondence. A letter, which has already been quoted in part, may mark a change in his decisions. It was written by Frau von Kleist to Bethge after the death of her two grandsons in action:

FRAU VON KLEIST TO BETHGE: I am feeling a new involvement in the terrible events. One does not want to be somehow shut out from all that has come upon us as an inexorable fate and guilt. And that, if I may say so, is what makes me for the first time uncertain about the course which you and Dietrich are taking at this time. Are we not all part and parcel of this intricate business, and ought we not, without balancing things too nicely, to take our spiritual forces into action where things are being fought out? Should we not go on our way more forcefully if we did not avoid this last contact?

G.S.II p. 408

That was 24th August, 1941. The effect of this letter can be seen in much of Bonhoeffer's writing at the time. One way to judge the effect is to study two circular letters he wrote to the Finkenwalde students, before and after. It was his custom to keep all informed about the death of their fellow-students. These lists lengthened as the war drew on, particularly the war in Russia. On 15th August, 1941, his circular letter read:

BONHOEFFER TO THE BRETHREN: Today I must tell you that our brothers Konrad Bojack, F. A. Preuss, Ulrich Nithack and Gerhard Schulze have been killed in the east. Konrad Bojack was with us in the summer of 1935. He was pastor in Lyck (East Prussia), where he leaves a wife and two small children. With the earnestness and joy of his faith, with his preaching, which was derived completely from God's word, with his love for the Church, for the ministry and for the community, he has been a good witness for Jesus Christ to us all. Born in Silesia, and making his home in East Prussia, the problems and needs of the German border country were particularly near to his heart. He proved his love for the homeland in being a faithful pastor to his community. He recognized his task and the salvation of his community in authentic preaching of Christ. He was killed on 22nd June, close to the East Prussian border. We mourn the loss of this tranquil, upright brother. In this life he trusted in the word and the sacrament. May he now see what he believed.

F. A. Preuss was with us at the same time as Konrad Bojack. He was a pastor in Landsberger Holländer in the Neumark, where he leaves a wife and two small children. He was always a friendly and joyful brother, who stood firm in faith in Jesus

Christ and who faithfully looked to the task appointed for him, in difficult circumstances. He served his community with great love and affection. Now Christ has called him to his heavenly community.

Ulrich Nithack was with us in the summer of 1938. No one who met him could miss the joy which emanated from him and the inner confidence which his faith in Christ had given him. His never-failing readiness to help the brothers, gratitude for the smallest thing, brought him the love of all the brothers. For him the work of a personal life in sanctification through Jesus Christ developed from a faith which was childlike in the best sense. Prayer was always the central thing for him. In a certainty that strengthened us all he saw that his way and his task lay completely within the Confessing Church, which he loved with all his heart. He gave himself completely to any work he was asked to do. With his death, something of the light of Jesus Christ that can be seen here and there among men has been quenched, to shine all the more brightly in the eternal sun of Jesus Christ.

Like Ulrich Nithack, Gerhard Schulze was with us in the summer of 1938. He came from working in a community which involved him in hard struggles, and he had stood boldly and clearly for the Church's cause. In his lively, warm and winning way he quickly found friends and fellowship wherever he was. He wanted to dedicate his life completely to the struggle of the Confessing Church. In a special way, God led him through depths and heights; he was able to experience the power of the grace of God in his life more powerfully than most. He wanted to carry on his ministry in the future in the light of this experience. His death affects many friends who went through life with him. A life so rich in grace does, however, fill us anew with the certainty that God's mercy has no end.

Apart from these brothers, who were particularly close to us through our work together, others have been killed: Hans-Otto Georgii, the brother of Wolf Georgii, who was with us in the winter of 1937–8 and whom we should remember particularly; Martin Franke from Pomerania, Engelke from Brandenburg, Heise from Saxony, and Nicolaus from the Rhineland. Some of you will remember from my confirmation class Hans Friedrich von Kleist-Retzow and his brother Jürgen Christoph, from Stettin. Both were killed in the east. An open copy of the New Testament was found beside Hans Friedrich.

They have gone before us on the way that we must all tread one day. God reminds those of you who are at the front in a specially gracious way to be prepared. We will watch over you with unceasing prayer. Of course you, and all of us, will be called by God only at the hour which God has chosen. Until this hour, which lies in God's hands alone, we will all be preserved, even in supreme danger, and our thankfulness for such preservation should lead us to constantly renewed preparedness for the last call.

Who understands the choice of those whom God takes to himself early? Does it not seem to us again and again in the early deaths of Christians as though God were robbing himself of his best instruments at a time when he needed them most? But God makes no mistakes. Does God perhaps need our brothers for some hidden service for us in the heavenly world? We should restrain our human thoughts, which always seek to know more than they can, and keep to what is certain. God has loved anyone whom he has called. 'For his soul was pleasing to the Lord, therefore he took him quickly from the midst of wickedness' (Wisd. 4. 14). We know that God and the Devil are locked together in combat over the world and that the Devil has a word to say even at death. In the face of death we cannot say in a fatalistic way, 'It is God's will'; we must add the opposite: 'It is not God's will.' Death shows that the world is not what it should be, but that it needs redemption. Christ alone overcomes death. Here, 'It is God's will' and 'It is not God's will' come to the most acute paradox and balance each other out. God agrees to be involved in something that is not his will, and from now on death must serve God despite itself. From now on, 'It is God's will' also embraces 'It is not God's will'. God's will is the overcoming of death through the death of Jesus Christ. Only in the cross and resurrection of Jesus Christ has death come under God's power, must it serve the purpose of God. Not a fatalistic surrender, but living faith in Jesus Christ, who died and has risen again for us, can seriously make an end of death for us.

In life with Jesus Christ, death as a universal fate which comes to us from outside is contrasted with death from within, one's own death, the free death of dying daily with Jesus Christ. Anyone who lives with Christ dies daily to his own will. Christ in us gives us over to death so that he can live in us. So our inner dying grows up against death from the outside. In this way, the Christian accepts his real death; physical death in the true sense does not become the end, but the consummation of life with Jesus Christ. Here we enter the community of the one who could say at his death, 'It is accomplished'.

Dear brothers, it may be that you now have little time or inclination for such thoughts. There are times in which all reality is so mysterious and oppresses us so much that any direct word seems to destroy the mystery of God for us, that we speak about and would like to hear about the last things only in hints. Everything that we can say about our belief then seems so flat and empty against the reality which we experience and behind which we believe there is an unspeakable mystery. It is the same with those of you at the front as it is with us at home: whatever is uttered vanishes in a flash, all formulas no longer make contact with reality. There can be something very real in all this, as long as one word does not vanish within us, namely the name of Jesus Christ. This name remains a word, the word around which we gather all our words. In this word alone lies clarity and strength. 'Within my heart abiding, thy name and cross alone my every thought are guiding, to bring me to thy throne.'

Let me end with a request. I know that some of you at the front and here are worried by thoughts about the future of our calling. Let these thoughts rest for a while. So far you have been able to give a good witness for our Church, even to suffer for our brothers. Let us not obscure anything now. We need this bit of earthly light and we shall need it still more. Who can ignore the fact that with this war we have been granted an interval which we really cannot bridge with our thoughts? So we should wait patiently.

Any letter, any token of life from you of course delights me and many others with me. I had greetings from brothers Bojack and Nithack just before their deaths, and I'm particularly glad of those today. Please let me know about changes of address as soon as possible. Often something – a book or a letter – comes back undeliverable. I'm always sorry then because a link has been broken. In that case it's usually very difficult to get the right address again.

I commend you to him who can preserve you by day and night, who can give you power in all your service, who will lead you and all of us to his kingdom.   G.S.II pp. 573–8

And then, after Frau von Kleist's letter had been re-echoed by further events, he wrote on 22nd November, 1941:

BONHOEFFER TO THE BRETHREN: I have to let you know now that our dear brothers Christoph Harhausen, Gunther Christ, Wolfgang Krause (Anhalt) and Johannes Staedler have been killed in Russia and that Joachim Staude has been missing since August. Brothers F. E. Schroter, H. D. Pompe, Winfried Krause, G. Seydel, G. Biesental have been wounded. It is difficult for me to write this to you. It is God's will to tear particularly large gaps in the ranks of the young pastors and so to lay a special burden on us. With our fallen brothers we lose fellow-workers in the struggle for a Church which is to serve only the Lord Jesus Christ. Every single one of them had to be in his community through particularly hard times, and experienced all the difficulties and all the blessings of a faithful ministry. In a few years, God has shown them what it means to be the shepherd of a community, and today we believe that in this way God wanted to prepare them for an early death. The uncertainty about Joachim Staude is especially hard. We should ask for God's presence and timely help for this quiet, always friendly and patient brother, firm in his faith. Christoph Harhausen continually strengthened and gladdened us by his joyful confidence for the cause of our Church, by his straight speaking and action. Gunther Christ showed himself faithful in many difficult situations in the community, and was a good brother to us in his firm, warm way. Wolfgang Krause came to us from his home province for church reasons. In his utterly upright and open character he was concerned for the clarity of the Church's cause and the message of Jesus Christ. One could not be with Johannes Staedler without being touched by his great love for Jesus Christ and his community. His last greeting to his wife was 'Glory and Hallelujah to our Lord and Saviour Jesus Christ'. Gunther Christ leaves a fiancée. W. Krause and J. Staedler were recently married. Our thoughts go out to those who have been robbed of the highest good fortune of their earthly life by death, and we do not forget the relatives of our departed brothers Bojack, Preuss, Nithack, G. Schulze, Kahn and Maass.

It happens that the passage of time, at first, at any rate, makes the departure of a well-loved person even more grievous. A daily sense of loss comes on top of grief. The less the names of our departed ones are mentioned, the more clearly an inner voice utters them to us from day to day. Who has not known the secret wish, that we could have taken their place?

How often have we been struck with horror when we think of the loneliness of their death? Why could we not have done the last brotherly service for them? Brother Heise, the brother-in-law of W. Schrader, was able to die in the presence of a brother with the words 'I am comforted'. But has not Christ all power richly to make up for the distance of all human help from one of his followers with his holy and gracious presence? Has he not heard what no human ear could hear, that 'I am comforted', sounding also in the hearts of those who died alone, yet with him. A great number of young preachers of the gospel have now gone. But the word that they have preached here as God's word is still alive, it lives in the believing community, it continues to have effect, it creates faith and brings forth fruit for the last day. Our brothers' lips are silent on this earth, but they laud and praise, now and for all eternity, the name of him who holds the kingdom, Jesus Christ. 'From men and from angelic voices be glory given to thee alone.'

Each of us has been involved in the war in different posts. The dimensions of this war are so immeasurable. There is an enormous difference, depending on whether one experiences the war fighting in the front line, as officer or in the ranks or as medical orderly or as chaplain, whether one is ordered to some service behind the front line, without the possibility of proving oneself specially, of special experience or distinction, whether one does one's service quietly in the homeland, or whether one has one's place assigned in a distant land. No one is of course spared the hours when his life seems senseless and his time wasted, in which he cannot share the awful experience of war in the very front line. Some letters from brothers who are behind the front in some apparently useless service reflect that. But there is a serious danger here of which we must become aware. There is danger, experience and testing in every moment for the Christian who knows what his faith is about, wherever he may be. If God in his pure grace grants to our brothers who are fighting, being wounded and dying in the very front line that even these particularly uncanny experiences should become blessings, it would be irreverent to this miracle to desire such experiences unasked for, and for oneself. Who knows how he would bear up? Who will conjure up God's miracle? But God knows what he can demand of us and he will indeed demand it of us in his own time. We should be ready for this hour, by accepting every day, quietly and faithfully, the measure of danger and proving that falls to our lot. I almost feel it to be robbing our brothers at the front when someone wants the indescribable lot which is theirs for himself.

We should also remember that being a man is ultimately not a matter of this or that experience, but of 'keeping God's word, being loving and being humble before one's God'. We may not belittle the task which comes daily from God through wishes and fantasies. If one or other of you today is still allowed 'to lead a quiet and peaceful life in all blessedness and reverence', i.e. in the service of Jesus Christ, in the midst of the world's tumults, that too is a miracle of God which equally belongs to the unsuspected dimension of the war and which is full of importance and promise for the war and for the brothers at the front. It is precisely the letters from the front which confirm that again and again. Anyone who is allowed to be in this position has one of the most important tasks to perform, to preserve that tranquil and quiet life for the day when the brethren return home, like the fire on the hearth which must not be allowed to go out. Here, as at the front, the important thing is complete faithfulness to the divine commission. Yet we live, here or there, not from our faithfulness, but again and again only from the forgiveness of our sins.

I have been struck, by reading about it in so many letters from the front, how the Bible, and even meditation, go with you right into the shell craters. We are grateful to you for that. It is a stimulus, a comfort, a humiliation and a help for us. Thank you for each word that we hear from you, for each prayer that is made for us. Let us enter into the last days of the Church's year with open hearts and again be certain and glad of the future of our Church.

The letter was left to lie, as I had to cope with inflammation of the lungs for several weeks. Now Edgar Engler and Robert Zenke have also been killed. It is very, very sad. These two men from Pomerania meant a great deal for the province in their steadfast attitude to the Church. They also knew that they were particularly responsible for the brotherhood and served it faithfully. Both had unlimited joy and great seriousness, which came from the same source, faith in Jesus Christ. Now we know that our brothers are with the one whom they served here in accordance with his calling. We should rejoice about that, despite all our sadness.

God bless you!   G.S.II pp. 578–82

The hindrances placed in the way of his work, the mounting casualties in the Russian campaign and his serious doubts about any other way to be rid of Hitler than by assassination, the development of his own theology, particularly in the field of ethics, all led him to involvement. He had not returned from America to be protected. As his former students died in Russia he was led deeper into the con-

spiracy which involved Josef Müller and his brother-in-law Hans von Dohnanyi with the military plot. Bonhoeffer had already shown some optimism after the advance in Russia of 22nd June, 1941, but the incredible successes had undermined the conspirators. Now the event which decided him was the first mass deportation of Jews on 16th October, 1941. The first clear evidence of his involvement in conspiracy is in his connection with 'Operation 7'. It was a small affair, but fatal for Bonhoeffer, and after it he was committed to conspiracy. Although small, it involved many difficulties with German and Swiss authorities. It was not successfully completed until the summer of 1942. The idea was to get a few Jews away from the horrors of the evacuation and mass deportations. The Abwehr *claimed that they needed Jews for their propaganda work in Switzerland. A handful of trusted Jews were to be sent to Switzerland to assure the Swiss that there was no persecution of Jews in Nazi Germany. At first, some of the Jews, misunderstanding the plan, refused to co-operate and they needed to be told that it was a plot and that they were not required to do anything for the Nazis! Then the Swiss had to be persuaded. Dr W. Rott consulted with Bonhoeffer, ill at the time, before sending the following request to the Federation of Swiss Churches:*

ROTT TO THE FEDERATION OF SWISS CHURCHES: On behalf of the chairman of the provisional governing body of the German Evangelical Church, Herr Superintendent Albertz, I beg to address to you, as President of the Federation of Swiss Churches, and so to the Churches themselves, a request as sincere as it is urgent.

It is a question of the extreme distress in which many of our non-Aryan brothers and sisters have been for some weeks . . . Since about the middle of October, the practice has been started of transporting to the east non-Aryans from Berlin and other towns. The whole matter confronts the Christian

Churches with questions and needs in the face of which we are almost entirely helpless.

We know that your hands, too, are almost tied. Reception of the directly threatened non-Aryan Christians into Switzerland seems impossible in view of the attitude of the police towards foreigners, and for other reasons; that was confirmed lately by Professor Courvoisier of Geneva . . . What we now ask you is whether, by urgent representations and official action by the Swiss Churches, the door might possibly be opened for just a few, or at least for one solitary case for which we specially plead . . .

There follows an account of the Friedenthal case, and Inge Jacobsen and Dr Emil Zweig are also included in the request:

It would be of great value, and might lessen the danger, if those concerned could soon have word (by telegram) that their immigration into (or transit through) Switzerland is arranged . . . We ask God, the Father of the forsaken, to show us a way out of all this dire distress. (*Quoted by Eberhard Bethge, from the archives of the World Council of Churches, and dated 'Berlin, October 1941'.*)

A letter from Bonhoeffer to Christoph Bethge about that time shows something of his mind that autumn.

17th November, 1941

BONHOEFFER TO CHRISTOPH BETHGE: It really was a great surprise which you . . . gave me . . . with your parcel. I would love to see you again and hear you talk. Now you're having your own experiences, and they are so completely different from those which I had at your age. I think that a great deal depends on what one experiences about the age of twenty, and above all, on how one takes it. For me, those were the years round 1926. Studies were coming to an end; one could learn and work in complete freedom; one travelled, and saw something of Europe. Europe was at that time recovering so gradually from the poverty, the divisions, the hatred, which the World War had brought. Germany was once again beginning to make a place for herself in the world through work, scholarship, intellect. Old prejudices of the nations against each other were giving way to a hope springing up among the Western peoples for a better, more fruitful, co-operation in the spirit of peace. The best popular forces were struggling to gain peace – a struggle which, of course, was hampered from the start. One could detect something like a task for the West, indeed a mission in the world. People worked and thought they knew why. Responsible, spiritually responsible, circles developed. We discussed passionately – against, but still, in the end, with, each other.

I could go on for a long time, and you will understand that I am to some extent emotionally involved in these reminiscences. But I also understand that this world has vanished, as far as you are concerned. You'll say, illusions, romanticism, dreams. You'll see other things, and perhaps think that what you see and experience now is the real world – just as we thought then. One will be as right and as wrong as the other. Perhaps one could say: today you are so completely occupied with the present that you have little inclination, and perhaps little strength, too, to think of the future, to plan; we were so completely occupied with the future in many respects that we made false judgements about the present. Now I believe that both will be equally necessary before long: men who see the present soberly, and yet still do not let the future – which is also part of reality – escape. Irresponsibility towards the future is nihilism, irresponsibility towards the past is enthusiasm. We must go beyond both, and in this task – which is also a highly personal one – we must, and can, once again unite ourselves, different though the background of our experiences may be. My firm conviction and indeed my experience in conversation with a number of people is that no man can look the present firmly in the eye today and at the same time have strength for future tasks unless he believes in the Creator – and the Redeemer . . . It would be splendid to talk about that again. Perhaps we would discover that we are talking about the same thing in very different words, and have the same end in view. Now enough of that. Goodbye, C. God bless you, wherever you are. With all best wishes.   G.S.II pp. 414–15

The correspondence which Bonhoeffer had with Eberhard Bethge and with his brother Christoph during 1942 is a preparation for the better known letters from prison. They show Dietrich thinking through some of the great and little problems of being a Christian minister in Wartime:

Kieckow, 14th December, 1941
BONHOEFFER TO EBERHARD BETHGE: Heartfelt greetings on the third Sunday in Advent. I hope to be there again on the fourth. We must practise the cantatas some more. How are things with the brethren? There will be plenty to talk about. Herr von Kleist is still laid up with his gall-stones. Tomorrow I'm going to Reimer. Frau von Kleist is coming on the 17th . . . All the best!

In the train to Munich, 18th June, 1942
BONHOEFFER TO EBERHARD BETHGE: I'm trying to put down some thoughts about John (the Evangelist) . . .

I hope I've helped you a bit with these remarks. You have a difficult time in front of you and I would very much like to give you some help in it.

Another couple of words about your sermon recently. I

have the impression, afterwards, that you are rather worried about the 'present reference' of the sermon. I understand this anxiety well, but I think you've got to the stage when you no longer need to be anxious. You're hardly likely to have lapses in this direction. You're reading a great deal of good stuff, and know more of the world than many others. Why shouldn't it be put with complete freedom in the service of the cause? Why should one's knowledge of human problems and problems in general not show from time to time? That means that the hearer is encouraged when he sees that his questions aren't simply overlooked and misunderstood. It was interesting for me to see that the starting point for the conversation after your sermon was the passage about the list of sermons of thirty years ago on this text. Do you remember? So I think that you can be rather freer.

The same goes for the personal sphere; there, too, one should not be over-anxious about the dangers of pietism. If a man is certain of his cause, he need not have these worries. Don't misunderstand me: I don't want your sermons to be 'modern' or pietistic, but I would like to relieve you of unnecessary hesitations in this direction. You really don't need to have them.

The journey is pleasant and attractive. It's a long time since I travelled through all these fine cities, whose cathedrals one knows, by day. It was a great joy. I thought of many experiences together, and the future of Germany has become even more important to me.

Goodbye. God be with you and your work.

P.S. Please send on the letter to C. It's a mad impression when one goes through the train and sees perhaps two or three people reading a book. Is that the great weariness, the great foolishness, a picture of the future? Almost all the people sitting in the train are young!

In the train to Munich, 18th June, 1942

BONHOEFFER TO CHRISTOPH BETHGE: A couple of days ago E. told me that it was your birthday today. I wanted to write to you for it. But I've only had a quiet moment for it on this journey. While I'm going through ancient cities and the summer countryside in the glorious sunshine, I keep thinking of you, your present life, and your future. What shall I say? What sort of thoughts and wishes can I have for you? In years you are half a generation, and in the rush of time at least a generation, younger than I. You experience, and think, and do, things which I never experienced or did or thought. You face dangers which I do not know. I live a life which is hardly like yours at all, and which must be strange to you. And yet it is this long journey, through our fine country, looking at the cathedrals of Naumburg, Bamberg, Nuremberg, at the cultivated fields which are sometimes so poor, and the thought that all this has been work and joy for many, many generations, that gives me confidence that here there is still common ground, a common task, a common hope, something which overcomes the gap between the generations. When one thinks of that, one's own short personal life becomes relatively unimportant; one begins to think in terms of greater periods and tasks.

At the moment, you are a member of a community which is in any case playing an active part in one of the great turning points of history. You yourself can hardly do anything to affect the whole course of events, probably you often feel yourself quite superfluous, out of place; you have all sorts of personal griefs and struggles. What else could I wish for you today but that you should learn not to take these little personal things, wishes and difficulties too seriously, but should understand that in your position, and in the possibilities given to you, you are a link in the long chain of these generations, which have worked and lived, and still work and live, for a fine, true and – faithful Germany. It is not the case that you can do nothing at all – even if it is less what you do than what you are that matters here. How tremendous the tasks will be once the struggle is no longer waged outside, when all our resources can be used for internal reconstruction! For that work, one day we shall need not only contributions and skills, but above all true men. And if you can only understand that God is using the present part of your life to make out of you a man whom he will later use, and set to work with all his capabilities and gifts, then you've already gained a great deal! And now it's probably important that those of us who are not being used fully at the moment should feel fully involved – and here too we have a common experience – in letting this time prepare us for one to come. It may be quite good for us to be put on one side, regarded as unimportant, for a time. That can teach us modesty and patience, and indeed faithfulness. And if God also wants to make faithful men of us at this time, whom he can use one day, then we should be very grateful to him for this time. – Now God preserve you in body and soul.

In the train to Munich, 25th June, 1942
BONHOEFFER TO EBERHARD BETHGE: Once again, a greeting from this train. I'm thinking of your work daily, and would so much like to hear how everything has gone . . . I'm now flying in the morning and coming back with Hans on the 10th (not the 9th). Where are you then? I've written to Frau von Kleist and invited myself for about 20th July . . . I'm also hoping that Thude's brother-in-law is leaving enough time with his massage. So something is certainly on until September. Christel should tell him once again; I don't think it's so good and effective if Thude does it himself.

My recent activity, which has been predominantly in the

secular sphere, keeps making me think. I'm amazed that I live, and can live, all day long without the Bible. If I were to force myself to it, I would regard my action, not as obedience, but as auto-suggestion. I understand that such auto-suggestion could be, and is, a great help, but I would be afraid in this way of falsifying a real experience and ultimately not finding any authentic help. When I open the Bible again, it is new, and more cheering than ever, and I would love to preach just once more. I know that I need only open my own books to hear what can be said against all this. I don't want to justify myself, but I recognize that 'spiritually' I have had much richer times. I detect that a rebellion against all things 'religious' is growing in me. Often it amounts to an instinctive horror – which is certainly not good. I'm not religious by nature. But I have to think continually of God and Christ; authenticity, life, freedom and mercy mean a great deal to me. It is just their religious manifestations which are so unattractive. Do you understand? These are no new ideas and insights, but as I believe I'm going to have a knot unravelled here, I'm letting these things have their head and not resisting them. That's the way in which I understand my present activity in the secular sphere. Excuse these confessions; blame the long railway journey. We ought to be able to talk about these things again in peace.

I haven't written to Maria . . . Goodbye . . . All the best. P.S. It's just a week since I was travelling in the same train; on an average, one person in each carriage was reading a book. Most people are dozing, just about half-awake. They're certainly almost all people who come from hectic activity. All they have for a couple of hours of leisure is a brooding to themselves, neither happily nor unhappily – it's like a more or less apathetic expectation of something in the future after one has done all that is in one's power; but at the same time it is neither surrender nor rebellion or defiance – their faces show a weary indifference instead. Their personal inner life has no more focus. Concentration on a book seems to belong to a past time.

Berlin, 18th September, 1942

BONHOEFFER TO HIS PARENTS: . . . In the meantime I've had confirmation from Munich that I need 'rooms for sleeping and working', i.e. two rooms . . . I shall go to Munich at the end of the coming week and do my two journeys from there, so I'll be away for about six weeks. If Berlin is not attacked until after the next full moon, we needn't count on it any more . . .

Berlin, 24th September, 1942

BONHOEFFER TO HIS PARENTS: . . . Stalingrad seems to be a frightful battle. It's very depressing for everyone and gets on one's nerves. They'll be needing continual reinforcements of officers and men . . .

Munich, 10th October, 1942

BONHOEFFER TO HANS-WALTER SCHLEICHER: I've just heard that you are to be called up next Thursday. Unfortunately I won't be able to see you before then. So I want at least to send you a brief note. We've often spoken recently about your being a soldier – sometimes in fun, but often in earnest.

Now it's happened, now that it's no longer a matter of possibilities, reflections, free decisions, but of an actual fact, in the face of which there are no more reflections and possibilities, most things all at once seem different. First of all, I would like to say that I'm really glad that the time of uncertainty and waiting is now over and that you can have the inner tranquillity of being where your contemporaries are; it was probably that which chiefly bothered you, and it will probably be that too which will give you inner help in difficult situations.

Not to want to be separate from the fate and need of other men, to want to have their companionship, is something quite different from simply wanting to join in, to go along with it; one should probably be on one's guard against 'wanting to experience' the war and its horror, for what person with that desire, in a light-hearted moment, knows how he stands in the hour of decision? But to be called, to take part in the fellowship, to contribute one's part and to share in the situation, whatever it may be, is, I feel, quite firm ground on which to stand and get through difficulties. And if one becomes conscious of this from time to time and in the end can live completely from the consciousness that this call is by no means a chance one, but that it is the way of God with one's life, one can, I believe, go very confidently out into the unknown. However, in that case quite definite, impenetrable barriers are set to life in the new community, and inwardly everything collapses for one if one destroys these boundaries out of a false solidarity.

You are not going into the army in the same way as most of your contemporaries. You've acquired a set of values and certain basic concepts of life. You know – perhaps still partly unconsciously, but that doesn't matter – the high value of a good family life, good parents, law and truth, humanity, education and tradition. You've studied music for years, and recently read many books which will not go by without having left some trace on you – and finally, you also know in some way what the Bible, the Lord's Prayer and church music are; from all that you have a picture of Germany which you will never lose, that will go with you to war, and for which you will do battle, wherever you are and whoever comes against you. As a soldier, you are perhaps freer for that than the rest of us. But it is clear, and you know it yourself, that conflicts are ahead of you, not only with what is common to our nature, whose power will terrify you in the next few weeks, but also simply because you, coming from the family you do, are different from most other men, different right down to the smallest external characteristics. The only important thing is that one regards one's advantages over others – and you have those! – not as deserved, but as a gift, and that one puts oneself with all that one has completely at the service of others and loves them despite their otherness.

We shall miss you a great deal, though we hope that we shall still have you here often and for a long time. You will certainly have a fine evening together on Wednesday. I would love to be there. Now goodbye, may all go well with you, and have an enjoyable time! And if at other times I am sparing with such words, let me say to you today, God bless you.

Klein-Krössin, 7th November, 1942
BONHOEFFER TO HANS-WALTER SCHLEICHER: Today, just this short greeting with the booklet which perhaps you can read some time in a quiet five minutes. Have you begun to learn and speak some French? That will be a great help. The horrible November weather probably doesn't help your acclimatization. But I think that now you are tougher in these things than we were at your age. By the way, if you really are homesick – I know it well enough, it's no disgrace – you must tell yourself that it's simply an ordinary illness which some people get and others don't, which has its crisis and its end and lasts for two or three weeks at most; perhaps you also don't know that it's something quite different from a bit of longing for home. It really is a grievous sickness, something very remarkable – but one can be sure that it will pass, like fever. I hope all goes well. Use the time as well as possible, and write if you need anything.

Berlin, 27th November, 1942

BONHOEFFER TO BETHGE: Recently I've very much missed being able to talk to you. The days have been so busy and my thoughts so unclear that I couldn't get down to writing . . . I was with Frau v. W. from Tuesday to Wednesday afternoon . . . Gist of the conversation: a year of complete separation . . . My answer: a year today was as good as five years, it meant a postponement into the unforeseeable future; I understood and recognized the right of the mother over the daughter, circumstances themselves would show whether such a rule could be carried out; I didn't believe it, and would talk about it again sometime . . .

I'm still not clear what to do next; don't say anything at the moment, there's no hurry now; first the storm must die down a bit. I think that I could have my way if I wanted to . . .

Otherwise everything is going on normally, i.e. things are still very bad with Winfried M., and it looks as though he won't get back again. Hans C. and his wife are getting better all the time. Your mother recently wanted to discuss family matters with John, who has become somewhat brusque, so nothing came of it. Besides, I have the impression that your mother is not well; she is quite at her wits' end with nerve trouble. By the way, I went back via Stettin and had a nice afternoon with Fritz and Margret. She's going to Kade for a fortnight, at the end of the week.

That's the latest news from home. I hope I'll hear from you soon. I'm thinking of your work.

Berlin, 29th November, Advent 1, 1942

BONHOEFFER TO BETHGE: It's midnight on the first Sunday in Advent. It was a lovely day. Morning prayers with S. on the *Magnificat*, lovely hymns later. I'm thinking of you and your work. We've usually celebrated Advent together in recent

years. How lovely the Advent music was at Sigurdshof! . . .
What are your thoughts for the year? . . .

Nothing new about the family. Hans is back; he's not
altered much. Sepp is very cheerful again and lively, and
hopes to be finished with his work in four weeks at most.
Unfortunately things aren't very good with Winfried. Renate
is doing a lot of work. Klaus comes often. There's no point in
going on to Margret, as she's in Kade, so you'd better come
here again. There will be lots to discuss if my silence over
personal matters hasn't in the meantime become second nature.
So enough for today. I hope to be able to get down to writing
again at last tomorrow.   G.S.II pp. 416–27

*During that same year he was involved in a theological controversy
about baptism. The Council of Brethren of the Church of the Old
Prussian Union had asked Bonhoeffer to defend the faith against a
Silesian pastor, Arnold Hitzer. Hitzer had attacked the practice of
infant baptism in no uncertain terms. He had said, 'Baptism depends
upon faith . . . It is the seal of justification by faith . . . Faith is the
personal faith of the baptismal candidate . . . Infant baptism cannot
be reconciled with the teaching of the Holy Scriptures about baptism.'
Bonhoeffer was given precise instructions and responded with the
following minor thesis:*

ON THE QUESTION OF BAPTISM

A. THE EVIDENCE OF HOLY SCRIPTURE

The *practice* of infant baptism cannot in fact be directly demonstrated in the New Testament (NT), but it nevertheless seems
to be probable in the light of it. In any case, its existence and
its justification cannot be disputed on either exegetical or
theological grounds.

I *Exegetical*

Matthew 28. 19. To take *baptizontes* with *matheteusate* ('teach them *and* baptize them', instead of 'teach them *by* baptizing them'; Hitzer deliberately adopts Luther's translation here and points to the significance of the word order) is indeed linguistically possible, but by no means conclusive. The ancient reading *baptisantes* ('teach them, after you have baptized them'; it occurs in the important manuscripts B and D), which according to Bengel's rule (the more difficult reading is to be preferred) simply cannot be passed over, would exclude co-ordination. The possibilities of exegesis, that the *matheteuein* is accomplished in 'baptizing' and 'teaching', must remain open, as must the possibility that the baptism is here prior to the teaching. The *autous* ('baptize *them*', i.e. 'them' is masculine here in the Greek, whereas 'nations' is a neuter, so that it is difficult to refer the 'them' to the 'nations'. Hitzer concludes that the Gentiles are to be evangelized and that those among them who become disciples, i.e. those who through being instructed come to believe, are baptized) may mean that we have here a selected group from the nations; further conclusions cannot be drawn from it. To understand *matheteuein*, 'teach', exclusively as evangelization through preaching cannot be justified adequately on linguistic grounds.

Mark 10. 15. In the present context, one possible translation for *hos paidion*, and according to J. Jeremias (*Did the Earliest Christians Practise Infant Baptism?* pp. 25 ff.), indeed the most obvious translation, is 'as a child' (Hitzer translates here: '*like* a little child', and concludes that Jesus sees in the character of children a *picture*, through which he makes clear to adults the disposition with which one must approach God).

Mark 10. 14. Jesus promises the kingdom of God to children. *Toiouton* (Hitzer points out here that the translation can only run 'such', and not 'these' (*touton*)) does not mean that the promise refers to those who are childlike in disposition, but rather that the promise applies not only to those who are brought to Jesus here, but to all who are like them, i.e. all children, as with the beatitude about the poor (cf. Lohmeyer, *Markuskommentar*, pp. 202 ff.).

Acts 16. 40 does not mean that the 'brethren' belong to the house of Lydia, but at most that they are assembled there. (Hitzer disputes here that even young children were baptized in the house of Lydia.)

Acts 16. 15, 33; 18. 8; I Cor. 1. 16; in Acts 11. 15 we hear of the baptism of a whole house – note the *hapantes, holos, pas*. Apart from the improbability of the assumption that there were no small children in these houses, it is impossible to exclude the 'children' of the house in principle, as even grown children are included among the 'children'. So there remains only the question of age. There is no indication anywhere that the small children are not included in the house or that they were to be excluded at baptism. This idea is in fact improbable in view of the concept of the house, which signifies an undivided totality (cf. also Matt. 10. 13).

Colossians 2. 11. It would be inappropriate to call baptism *peritome tou Christou* if no infants were in fact baptized, as circumcision took place on the eighth day after the birth. There is no scriptural basis for the idea that the circumcision of children derived from their *natural* participation in the community of the Israelite *people*; it is much more a sign of the divine covenant which includes both father and children. Only for that reason can Paul call baptism *peritome tou Christou* and can circumcision play so great a role in theological controversy in the New Testament.

Acts 2. 38 . . . 'you and your children'. In view of the expectation of the imminent end of the world we are to understand 'children' to refer to the sons and daughters of those who are addressed rather than to the coming generations, cf. 2. 17. The eschatological character of baptism as a deliverance from the final judgement (2. 40) makes a differentiation in the age of the children improbable.

Remarks about children in general. John is filled with the Holy Spirit from his mother's womb (Luke 1. 15); in the meeting between Mary and Elizabeth 'the babe leaped in Elizabeth's womb' (Luke 1. 41). The newborn Jesus is the Lord and Saviour of the world (Luke 2. 10; 2. 30 f.). Children are 'brought to Jesus' (Mark 10. 13, and the same expression *prospherein* is used as in the healing miracles at 7. 32; 8. 22, i.e. in events of eschatological significance). The strong expressions – 'the disciples were bringing them', 'rebuked them' (cf. Mark 8. 33), Jesus was 'unwilling' (cf. Mark 7. 34), Jesus' call 'to suffer the children to come to him' (cf. Matt. 11. 28), not to 'hinder' them, taking the children in his arms (cf. Mark 9. 36 and Luke 2. 28) (it is therefore a question of very small children) – before the blessing which is desired indicate an event of eschatological significance (cf. Lohmeyer, ad loc.). The kingdom of God belongs to children (Mark 10. 13 f.); Luke 18. 15 has *brephe* (infants) instead of *paidia* (children from eight days to twelve years). There was no question of Jesus baptizing children, as baptism with the Holy Spirit only became possible after Jesus' resurrection and departure, and the baptism of John was superseded by the presence of Christ.

In Matthew 18. 1 a child is made an example for the disciples to follow, not in his disposition but in his nature. The acceptance of a child is equivalent to the acceptance of Christ (Mark 9. 37). In the Temple, children shout 'Hosanna to the Son of David', and in this Jesus sees the fulfilment of Psalm 8. 2 (Matt. 21. 15 f.). Here too the eschatological character of the event is clear. When the inbreaking kingdom of God, salvation, is mentioned in the NT, there is never a relegation of children into the background – on the contrary, an attempt of this sort by the disciples (!) is met by the indignation, i.e. the anger, of Jesus.

Jesus' acceptance of children, like his acceptance of the blind, the lame and the poor, is an eschatological saving event. It therefore does not happen on the basis of some natural innocence of children, psychologically understood – that is a completely modern idea – but as a miracle of God, who humbles the mighty and exalts the lowly. The 'innocence' of children is a gift of Christ, and never a natural characteristic, by virtue of which the gifts of Christ – for example, baptism – would be superfluous. The eschatological character of the acceptance of the children by Jesus rather demands their baptism through the Church.

Remarks about children in the Christian community. In Ephesians 6. 2 and Colossians 3. 20, children are addressed on the express presupposition that they belong to the community, *en kyrio*. (It is at least possible that I John 3. 12 and 14 also belong here.) Nowhere in the New Testament is it said that the unbaptized belong to the community. There is no indication, either, that children should be baptized at a particular age; there is no admonition to this effect either to parents or to children, and once again this can be most easily understood on the obvious presupposition of infant baptism. In any case, the 'argument from silence' can be advanced more strongly in favour of infant baptism than against it. I Corinthians 7. 14 speaks for infant baptism rather than against it. The idea that baptism is superfluous because of the 'holiness' of children is an impossible one in view of the fact that baptism is not only an act of the forgiveness of sins but also a 'sealing' for the final judgement (quite apart from the fact that a gift of God's grace is never 'superfluous' in the NT, otherwise it is quite possible that baptism would also be 'superfluous' for believers too). The holiness of children can be regarded as a precondition of their baptism, one which makes the question whether they are old enough quite unnecessary. References to Jewish proselyte law, according to which children born after the conversion of their parents need not be baptized because they are born 'in holiness', offer only a limited analogy, as even children like this were circumcised. And Christian baptism is *peritome tou Christou*. The idea that children who were born before the conversion of their parents had to be baptized, whereas children born of Christian parents were not baptized, leads to the improbable idea, for which there is no confirmation anywhere, of baptized and unbaptized both being members of the Christian community.

II *Theological*
Baptism and Faith in the NT. If infant baptism can be neither affirmed nor disputed on purely exegetical grounds, then perhaps a theological inference from other biblical statements will lead to a further clarification.

1. *Baptism and faith stand in an indissoluble connection in the New Testament*. Because of this, the objective character of the two should be stressed far more strongly than Hitzer does in his study. Baptism is the translation of a man into the eschatological community, incorporation into the body of Christ, which really takes place through a physical action ordained by Christ. In it there takes place the washing away of sins, being born again, dying and rising with Christ, receiving the Holy Spirit, being made one with the image of Christ, and being sealed in the eschatological community for the day of judgement. All this happens without any co-operation and activity on the part of men, as Christ's own action (Eph. 5. 26) in his community. Where there is any mention of the saving gift of

baptism, hardly any attention is paid to the individual who receives it or to the personal 'conditions' which are attached to the receiving of baptism; instead, all the weight falls on the power which is embodied in the sacrament when it is performed as ordained by Christ, a power which does not depend on any human conditions, and on the totality of the community, the body of Christ, to which this sacrament belongs. Indeed, I Corinthians 15. 29, despite all the desperate attempts to interpret it in another way, speaks of a baptism for the dead (probably Christians who died unbaptized). And not only does Paul have no objection against this custom, he even uses it as an argument against those who deny the resurrection. If baptism really means 'being born again', resurrection from the dead (cf. Rom. 6, and also Eph. 5. 14), why should not such a custom develop from this idea of baptism as an extreme expression of the power of the sacrament, even if it was not accepted by the Church? Investigations of Paul's thought in recent years have taught us to recognize this realism of Pauline thought more and more clearly, and have made it impossible for this thought to be translated into 'moral-spiritual' categories.

Now no one can fail to see that baptism is always associated extremely closely with faith (in addition to the passages already cited, see especially Rom. 6. 8, 11; Col. 2. 12b; Gal. 3. 26 ff.). Although it is never said in so many words that only believers can be baptized, the conjunction of baptism and belief is a tacit presupposition of all New Testament statements. Now of course, to begin with, the concept of belief needs to be clarified in some respects. The definition of belief (faith) as 'personal faith', 'personal decision for Jesus', 'free decision of the individual', which predominates in Hitzer's study, almost imperceptibly gives the biblical concept an alien colouring which must have doubtful consequences. At least, it must be noted that the formula 'my faith' or 'I believe' never occurs in Paul's writing (cf. the qualification of the 'I believe' in Mark 9. 24; Acts 8. 37 is a later, badly attested, addition according to Nestle), and that the noun 'faith', 'belief,' is far more frequent in Paul than the verb 'believe' (in Gal., e.g. 3. 22; cf. Lohmeyer, *Grundlagen der paulinischen Theologie*, pp. 115 ff.), that even 'we believe' or 'you believe' is relatively rare in contrast with the absolute use of the substantive and the important phrase *pistis Christou*. The formula 'faith came', 'faith was revealed' (Gal. 3. 23, 25) is particularly striking. So faith is to be regarded primarily in an objective sense as revelation, event, grace, gift of God (or Christ) through which the 'I' is completely done away with – 'I . . . , yet not I' (Gal. 2. 20!). In faith we participate in an event in which God is solely and totally the active one, as Father, Son and Holy Spirit (cf. I Cor. 12. 3; Rom. 8. 15, 26 f.). Only because 'faith came', 'was revealed', do *we* believe, as a community; and only when that is recognized can we say 'I believe', and even then with the qualification 'I believe – help my unbelief'. And again, even then, we must say it in such a way that attention is at no point drawn to the 'I', but to the content of belief. It will be already clear from this that the concept of faith which underlies Hitzer's study most unbiblically puts the emphasis on the personal element, on the 'I', on the free decision, and thus seriously burdens the problem of baptism and faith right from the start.

2. *Man is purely passive towards baptism.* There is no self-baptism, and even the middle 'have oneself baptized', which occurs so strikingly often in Hitzer's study, occurs only once in the NT (Acts 22. 16); otherwise we always have the passive. A man *is* baptized. The faith which receives baptism – and baptism can only be received in faith – cannot in any way be understood as active co-operation in baptism; it is pure receiving, and real only in the act of receiving itself. Faith is

not therefore an independent presupposition which could be detached from the receiving of baptism. Without faith there is no salvation, no fellowship with Christ. But faith does not create salvation and it does not create the sacrament, it receives it. Even in faith, or rather, precisely in faith, man is purely passive towards salvation; indeed, faith is virtually the theological term which describes the pure passivity of man in receiving salvation. So 'justification by grace alone' is the same thing as 'justification by faith alone'. 'There is no trace of the idea that the essence of faith is self-surrender to God and Christ in Paul or anywhere else in the New Testament' (Cremer: *Bibl.-theol. Wörterbuch*, 9th ed., p. 844).

3. *Faith always arises by the word of God (Romans 10. 17), so it can be represented in psychological terms only as a deliberate, comprehending hearing of, and response to, the word of God.* 'Confession of faith' and 'decision of faith' are – necessarily – expressions, forms of faith, but they are not identical with faith itself. There are confessions of Christ and personal decisions for Christ which could not stand before Christ (Matt. 7. 21; Luke 9. 57 ff.; Matt. 26. 33 ff.). The nature of faith is independent of our ability to present it in psychological terms! Faith is a theological, not a psychological, concept! – deliberate understanding, answering, decision, but purely the receiving of salvation as it has been manifested to us in Christ as the Word of God. The NT does not reflect further upon the psychological possibilities of this act of receiving. The NT is not interested in the predominant point of Hitzer's study. It speaks of the possibilities of receiving salvation only in hints, which never result in a personal confession of faith or a personal decision of faith. In Matthew 9. 2, Jesus promises forgiveness of sins to the paralytic because of the faith of those who bear him (even if *auton*, '*their* faith', is *also* meant to refer to the paralytic – and this is hardly possible linguistically – it is worth

noting that we do not have '*autou*', '*his* faith'; cf. the healing miracles which follow the faith and the intercessions of others, especially Mark 9. 23; Matt. 8. 13!). I Corinthians 7. 14 talks of a consecration of an unbelieving husband through a believer, which is not conditioned by personal faith. I Corinthians 15. 29 has a special place in this context, as does the promise of salvation to the infants (Luke 18. 15), and Jesus' praise and thanks for the revelation of God to the 'babes' (cf. also Luke 9. 49 f., where, immediately after the episode of the receiving of the child, John reports that they forbade a man who was doing miracles in Jesus' name because he was not a follower of Jesus – the common factor between this man and the children evidently consists in his not being a follower, not having made a conscious decision – and Jesus replies, 'Do not forbid him' (cf. Luke 18. 16), 'for he that is not against us is for us'). Finally, the corporate thought of the New Testament also belongs here (cf. Matt. 10. 13, and the words over the cities in Matt. 11. 20). The consequence of all these passages is no more, but also no less, than the justification of putting the question whether it is permissible to withhold baptism from children born of believing parents because they do not have the psychological potentialities of a personal confession and decision.

4. *The NT speaks expressly only of the baptism of believers.* Proclamation, repentance, faith, baptism is the sequence which is always attested. The person who has come to believe is incorporated into the body of Christ by baptism. So the practice of the NT offers a concrete solution of the problem of the actual relationship of baptism and faith by the dominant practice of adult baptism. This corresponds to the mission situation. But it would not be permissible, as we have seen, to understand the actual connection of baptism and faith *exclusively* as the temporal juxtaposition of a personal confession of faith and baptism. There is baptism only where there is

faith. In the mission situation, that means deliberate profession of faith by adults, but as even the profession of faith may not by its very nature be regarded as a work, as a psychical occurrence (besides, we have no certain evidence of it in any scriptural passage which deals with baptism), the question whether faith, as purely an act of receiving, cannot also be the representative faith of the community for its children, i.e. the faith of the infant children of the community itself, remains an open one. It should always be remembered in this context that a man is never baptized 'in' his faith, and so children are never baptized 'in' the faith of the community or their own faith; baptism is always in the name of Jesus Christ. The New Testament practice of the believing baptism of adults can be understood theologically only as one possible solution of the relationship of baptism and faith, alongside which the possibility of infant baptism cannot be excluded. In any case, the New Testament provides no grounds for the *refusal* of infant baptism, precisely because of the concept of faith which is to be found in the doctrine of justification. In addition to this insight, which has been won from the concept of faith, we also have Jesus' command and promise of baptism as a sacramental reality and the knowledge that each man is born in sin and needs to be reborn. So the theoretical possibility of infant baptism becomes a concrete hope in faith, a confidence, as a result of which the community feels that it can no longer withhold baptism from its children.

B. ON THE DOCTRINE OF THE LUTHERAN CONFESSIONAL WRITINGS

1. *The foundation of baptism is Christ's command to baptize.* This is universal. The gift of baptism is (summed up in the decisive concept) rebirth. The effectiveness of baptism rests on the

command and promise of Christ. Baptism demands faith as God's gift of grace. What are the consequences of that for infant baptism? How is infant baptism received in faith? Answer: through the faith of children and through the faith of the community.

2. *The faith of children:* The chief objection is directed at its psychological impossibility. To this, the following reply may be given:

(a) From a psychological point of view, it is no more difficult to speak of the *sin* of children, than to speak of the doctrine of original sin. Sin and faith are not psychological acts, but real relationships to God.

(b) The Reformers' concept of faith is not determined psychologically, like that of the Pietists, but theologically. 'Such faith', 'hang on' and 'grasp' refer simply to the receiving of grace in such a way that any psychological description of this event must be ruled out. Nor can this act of receiving be 'tied up with psychological preconditions' (Schlink, *Theologie der Bek. Schriften*, 213).

(c) The later Lutheran distinction between *fides directa* and *reflexiva, immediata* and *mediata,* is theologically justified, and protects the concept of faith from being described in psychological or legalistic terms.

(d) Luther makes no independent *theologoumenon* of infant baptism, but he refutes the false arguments which would assert its impossibility.

3. *The faith of godparents:* The main objection concerns the impossibility of representative faith. Here it must be argued that:

(a) The faith of the community always precedes the faith of the individual; it does so in two respects: first, because the community administers baptism in faith, at the command and promise of Christ, and secondly because the community receives baptism in faith, praying for the person being baptized.

(b) The faith of the community therefore claims Christ's word in intercession for the child and is certain that God will hear its prayer.

(c) The faith of the community does not baptize the child in the strength of the community's faith or that of its children, but in the power of the word of Christ.

(d) The faith of the community supports the children by intercession and Christian instruction on the basis of the baptism which has been administered.

(e) The community can no more see into the heart of the adult whom it accepts as a member, in faith, through baptism, on the basis of his confession, than it can into that of the child.

(f) The faith of the community is no work which it performs in the place of the child; it is intercession, hope, and acceptance of the promises of Christ for the child, brought about by the word of Christ.

(g) Claiming the Gospel of Mark 10. 13 ff. for infant baptism is a result of the promise which it contains that the kingdom of heaven is given to children. How could one refuse baptism to those to whom the kingdom of heaven belongs?

(h) The argument of the Confessional writings does not so much produce a positive dogmatic proof of the necessity of infant baptism as dispute the justification of refusing to baptize infants. Neither 'representative' faith nor the faith of children may be made an independent *theologoumenon*; the faith of the community in which it ventures to baptize children on the basis of Christ's promise is not contradicted, nor is it rejected as heresy by a biblicistic legalism.

(i) As far as the relationship of the faith of infants and the faith of godparents is concerned, it should be noticed that the Confessional writings mention the two side by side. Considerably more stress is put on the faith of the godparents, without which infant baptism is impossible. Here too, the faith of the community supports the faith of the individual. The unspoken faith of the child is publicly confessed by the godparents.

(j) In the end, the faith of children and the faith of godparents is simply an expression of the objectivity of faith which was spoken of in the context of the New Testament. Because '*faith* came', '*faith* was revealed', where the event has taken place, baptism may be administered and received in faith.

4. *Theological reflection must therefore, strictly speaking, restrict itself to opening up the possibility of infant baptism.* The doctrine of infant baptism is a peripheral doctrine which cannot be made the basis of systematic development, but it still has its rightful place. This inner limit to the possibility of making theological statements about infant baptism is exceeded (even in the Confessional writings) where an independent doctrine is put forward of the need of infant baptism for salvation, and of the damnation of children who die unbaptized. Where the concept of what is necessary for salvation is applied to individual aspects of the reality of revelation, by itself it leads to an intolerable fragmentation of the totality of salvation and to a legalistic understanding of the individual aspects. The biblical question is not what *must* necessarily happen for salvation, but what *may* happen. But with salvation at stake, who would refuse to do what he *might* do? It is never possible to give a direct answer to the question of the salvation of the dead, even where it is asked of those who have been baptized. It makes sense and is justified only because it keeps directing the individual and the community entirely to God's grace, i.e. to Christ, his word and his sacrament. The casuistry which has developed over the question whether baptism is necessary for salvation makes baptism a human work. But it is equally false to declare that infant baptism is unnecessary for the salvation of children,

and without further ado to appeal to a grace of God which is 'greater than baptism' (Hitzer, p. 18), of which no mention can be found in Scripture. In this context, the charge that the Confessional writings tie the grace of God too tightly to baptism and thus make baptism an independent factor alongside Christ must be rejected. One need not tell the authors of the Confessional writings in as many words that we are not saved through faith in baptism but through faith in Christ. But the Confessional writings have stressed with good reason that it has pleased God to 'tie' his grace to Christ – and that means to word and sacrament – and that there is no grace of God which would be revealed to us outside word and sacrament. The God who, according to our thoughts and wishes, is to be 'greater' than his grace is not the God of the Bible. Instead of looking for such a 'greater' God, about whom in any case we could know nothing, we are to praise and hold to his gracious presence as it has been given to us in its association with word and sacrament.

5. *The Confessional writings rightly resist the enthusiasts who forbade infant baptism.* On the contrary, they allow infant baptism on the basis of Scripture and of its 'key' – the doctrine of justification. But above all, they reject as enthusiastic arrogance the view that the baptism performed by the Church in faith in the word of Christ and in his name is no baptism. The *validity* of baptism rests solely on the command and the promise of Jesus Christ. The *benefit* of baptism depends on the faith of the person who receives it. So even the opponents of infant baptism may never question its validity, but at best the benefit it brings.

6. *The Confessional writings give no further information about the temporal relationship of baptism and faith.* They content themselves with establishing the essential connection between the two. Whereas in adult baptism faith temporally precedes

baptism, in infant baptism the question remains open. It is true that the faith of the community precedes the baptism, but the faith of the children and their later, conscious, faith are consequences of baptism. The faith of the present community is inconceivable without the institution of baptism which precedes it. Once again, the first community was itself baptized as believers. But in the end, the institution of baptism by Christ precedes the faith of the community as it was grounded in Pentecost. So in the last resort the question of the temporal relationship between baptism and faith (unless some definite point in time, say, for example, the baptism of the first community, is torn from its general context) amounts to the question of the temporal relationship of word to sacrament. But this question can no longer be settled theologically, as in Jesus Christ word and sacrament are one. John 1. 1 cannot be detached from John 1. 14. The argument that Christ preached first, and only instituted the sacraments at the end of his life, ignores the fact that the physical presence of Christ as he preached was itself already a sacrament, and that the institution of the sacraments before his departure can be understood only as an assurance of his continuing physical presence. So the question of the temporal relationship of word to sacrament, of faith to baptism, cannot be solved theologically, but only pedagogically, practically and psychologically. It is certainly impermissible – and here Hitzer's study is right – to infer the need for infant baptism, for example, from the dogmatic concept of *gratia preveniens*, to treat infant baptism as an illustration of a dogmatic principle. And of course it is equally impermissible to deduce the rejection of infant baptism from some particular concept of the community. Only the biblical statements about baptism, which are opened by the key of Holy Scripture, the message of justification by grace and faith alone, determine the rightness or wrongness of infant baptism.

If infant baptism is to be regarded as permissible on this authority, we may later introduce, for example, the concept of *gratia preveniens* as an illustration of infant baptism with perfect justification.

C. BAPTISM AND COMMUNITY

1. *Just as in the missionary situation the question of the relationship of baptism and faith is solved by the predominance of adult baptism, so in the situation of the popular Church it is solved by the predominance of infant baptism.* Both possibilities are given in the freedom and responsibility of the community, and are put into practice, depending on the spiritual situation of the community, the faith of the community, and its situation in the world. When infant baptism is practised without any firm relationship to the faith of the community, and when the faith of adults becomes a work on which the validity of baptism is to depend, baptism is equally misused. There is always a threat that infant baptism will detach baptism from faith, just as there is always a threat that adult baptism will destroy the grace of baptism which is grounded solely in Christ's word. A misuse of infant baptism (and such a misuse can without doubt be established in the past history of our Church) will therefore inevitably lead the community to an appropriate limitation of its use and to a new evaluation of adult baptism.

2. *Time and again, in periods when the Church is being secularized, complete rejection of infant baptism and the demand for believers' baptism and rebaptism become slogans for the renewal of the Church,* that is, for the formation of a pure community, set apart from the world. The Church has never been renewed by these slogans. Instead, the result has been countless splinter groups, some of which live a life of their own on the periphery of the Church and others of which have returned to infant baptism

in the second generation. This assertion is no theological argument; it belongs to the acts of church history which every responsible Christian who is concerned with these questions must consider.

3. *The speculative-historical assertion that infant baptism must come to an end with the end of the Constantinian epoch of church history in our days is based on the false assumption that infant baptism was first introduced under Constantine.* On the other hand, it is clear that Irenaeus, Tertullian, Hippolytus and Origen (who derives it from apostolic tradition) already presupposed infant baptism as a general practice. The synod of Carthage in 251 deliberated on the question whether children should be baptized on the third day or the eighth day after birth. The feature of the Constantinian age was not that the Christian community baptized its children, but that baptism as such became a qualification for civic life. The false development lies not in infant baptism but in this secular qualification of baptism. The two should clearly be distinguished.

4. *The desire for a community of believers set apart from the world, pure, authentic, truthful, capable of making sacrifices and joining in the struggle, is very understandable in a secularized Church, but it is full of dangers:* in this case, a community ideal too easily takes the place of the real community of God; the pure community is too easily understood as a contribution to be made by man; Jesus' parables about the tares in the field and the fish-net are too easily overlooked; it is too easily forgotten that God loved the *world*, and wills that *all* men should be helped; a narrow, legalistic biblicism too easily takes the place of a responsible theological approach. The separation of the community from the world, purity, readiness to fight, truthfulness, are not goals to be striven for directly, in themselves; they are the fruits which automatically follow from an authentic proclamation of the gospel. Luther's Reformation was not the result of an

attempt to realize a better, perhaps a 'primitive Christian', community ideal, but of a new knowledge of the gospel from Holy Scripture. In our days we cannot be concerned with the restoration of the primitive Christian community, but only with the communication of the gospel. True renewal of the Church will always be distinguishable from enthusiasm by the way in which it takes the central, assured doctrines of Scripture as its starting point. Now it is indeed indubitable that the right administration of the sacrament of baptism is a central demand of Scripture; on the other hand, after everything that has been said, the rejection of infant baptism certainly cannot be described as a central and assured doctrine of Holy Scripture. Now where human thoughts – even though they may be the best, the purest and the most devoted of human thoughts – are made the starting point for attempts to renew the Church, the Church's cause, which rests solely on the clear and assured word of God, is endangered, particularly if human thoughts reject the faith of the Church and give themselves out to be the sole divine truth.

5. The following formulations in the 'Special Consideration of Baptism and the Community' are *particularly suspect* (p. 39): 'Let anyone who does not whole-heartedly take Christ's side in confessing it and expressing it by having himself baptized remain outside! . . . Here a clear, total decision is demanded, the air is clear, this truthfulness makes the message credible and the Church's witness attractive for the young'!

This is the voice of a rigorism and idealism (which is indeed attractive to the young) which identifies personal decision all too directly with faith (see above), which quenches the dimly burning wick and breaks the bruised reed. The remark on page 38, that, from a subjective point of view, to belong to the community of Jesus Christ rests on the free decision of the individual, on free will, agrees with this. Here too, 'free decision' takes the place of 'faith' and thus leads to a dangerous distortion of the biblical concept of faith (see above). The introduction of the unbiblical concept of 'believers' baptism' and the use of the middle form ('have oneself baptized'), which recurs with striking frequency in contrast to the NT, corresponds to this alteration of the concept in terminology and thus at the same time in content. All this points in the direction of a psychological, activistic thought which is moving away from the Bible. 'Decision for Christ' – itself an unbiblical phrase – is the activistic perversion of the passive character of faith; decision for Christ puts man in the centre of the study. 'Faith' is directed wholly towards its object, towards Christ. On page 37, infant baptism is described as an attack not only on the freedom of man (and where does *this* concept of freedom come from? – from idealism and liberal theology, not from the Bible), but also on God in his gracious election. This is a denial of the universality of God's will to save as it is attested in Scripture; God's grace is separated from his means of grace (as we have already noticed in other places above) and the community and the world are eternally distinguished as the elect and the damned. But in that case, what about John 3. 16? The same relationship of community and world which was described earlier on the psychological level as 'personal decision' and 'irresolution' repeats itself here on the basis of an abstract doctrine of double predestination and, accordingly, of a freedom of God from his means of grace, i.e. from his revelation. In both cases the true relationship of the community to the world, which only develops in faith in the revelation of God in the world (and embraces both John 3. 16 and I John 2. 17), is neglected and wrongly formulated in too one-sided a way. This may be more impressive, and more attractive, but it makes the Church of God a pious ideal.

6. *The abolition of infant baptism is no effective way of combating*

the secularization of the Church, as even 'believers' baptism' is no guarantee against severe lapses; indeed, it is the special stress on personal experiences of conversion itself which has been shown by experience often to lead to enthusiastic deviations and reverses.

7. *The Christian community of today requires an authentic evangelical baptismal discipline rather than the abolition of infant baptism.* As infant baptism cannot be forbidden on scriptural grounds where it is performed in faith – i.e. within the believing community – but rather may be thankfully grasped as God's special gift of grace to the believing community, authentic evangelical baptismal discipline will have to consider whether or not believing godparents and parents are bringing the child to baptism as members of the community. In the first place, it will take baptismal instruction for the community, godparents and parents, more seriously than hitherto; it will bear witness to the special grace of infant baptism, which may not be dissipated; it will warn against the misuse of baptism and it will, if need be, refuse to baptize infants when it has come to the firm conclusion that baptism is not desired in faith. But it will not allow its refusal to be guided by any sort of rigorism, but only by the love of God for the world and for his community.

8. *What is the Church's attitude towards Christians who think that infant baptism must be rejected altogether on grounds of faith?*

(a) It has no right, on the basis of Holy Scripture, to discipline faithful members of the community who do not have their children baptized.

(b) The same is true of pastors who take the same standpoint with regard to their families. It will see in both cases a practical reference to the seriousness of baptismal grace.

(c) But it cannot allow its pastors to refuse baptism to any believing Christians who desire baptism for their children, because this refusal cannot be justified from Scripture.

(d) It cannot allow its pastors to preach the doctrine, contrary to Scripture, that infant baptism is not permissible, although it cannot prevent them from commending adult baptism on biblical grounds.

(e) Under no circumstances can it tolerate rebaptism, i.e. the declaration that the baptism of Christ's Church, performed from times immemorial in faith in the word of Christ, is invalid. To teach and to practise rebaptism destroys the unity and fellowship of the Church by regarding all those who were baptized when children as unbaptized and therefore as not belonging to the body of Christ. Those who are rebaptized separate themselves not only from the world, but also from the Church of Jesus Christ.   G.S.III pp. 432–54

This was Bonhoeffer's last official defence of the practice of the Church. He is uneasy throughout.

More typical of the man of 1942 was a letter written at the news of the death of three of his colleagues. The letter of 1st March, 1942, is a herald of his struggle and defence of the faith against circumstances. It is significant that he closes it with a quotation from Luther:

1st March, 1942

BONHOEFFER TO THE BRETHREN: Our dear brothers, Bruno Kerlin, Gerhard Vibrans and Gerhard Lehne, have been killed. Now they sleep with all the brothers who have gone before them, awaiting the great Easter-Day of the resurrection. We see the cross, and we believe in the resurrection; we see death, and we believe in eternal life; we trace sorrow and separation, but we believe in an eternal joy and fellowship. Bruno Kerlin was a witness to this Easter faith in the joy of his belief, the transparency of his character, his brotherly readiness to serve, and we thank God for it. Gerhard Vibrans was hit by a flying-bomb just as he was about to join companions in singing from the New Hymnal. Anyone who knew this pure, selfless brother, who combined simplicity and maturity so well that he won the confidence of all sorts of people, knows what we lost with him. The text of the day of his death, 3rd February, was particularly moving: Revelation 1. 14. The life of this brother stood under the 'flaming fire' of the eyes of Christ; he was a reflection of this glaring fire. I shall never forget how he taught me Claudius' hymn, 'I thank God and rejoice'. His life provided a most convincing exposition of it. Gerhard Lehne was a questioning, seeking, wandering, restless man, with many-sided experiences and interests, and also great boldness and simple honesty. The purpose by which he was grasped shone through everything. He served his Church in self-sacrificing faithfulness. Now God has brought him early to rest and peace. We praise and thank God for the life and death of our brothers. Their death reminds us of the blessing which God once gave us through fellowship at his word and table; we also hear the warning to be true to each other as long as we can.

I have experienced the signs of such faithfulness in an overwhelming way over the past weeks. I can never express my thankfulness for it in words. All through the month letters kept arriving for my birthday from people who are working hard in the homeland and also from the bitterest cold of Russia, some written in brief pauses in the action. How shall I respond to such faithfulness? I thank you from the bottom of my heart. Let us remain firm in prayer for each other. Who knows how much preservation he owes, through God's grace, to the intercession of a brother?

I was surprised to see how it has been recently that there has been an increase in the voices from the front and from home which ask for a new help to meditation. I confess that I would not have ventured to talk about that with you now on my own initiative. I didn't want to add yet one more burden to

those you already bear each day. So even today I will do no
more than say a few words once again about the precious gift
which is given to us in meditation, and in a way which is
particularly important for us today. Daily, quiet attention to
the word of God which is meant for me, even if it is only for a
few minutes, will become for me the focal point of everything
which brings inward and outward order into my life. In the
interruption and fragmentation of our previous ordered life
which this time brings with it, in the danger of losing inner
discipline through the host of events, the incessant claims of
work and service, through doubt and temptation, struggle and
disquiet of all kinds, meditation gives our life something like
constancy, it keeps the link with our previous life, from baptism
to confirmation, to ordination. It keeps us in the saving fellowship of the community, the brethren, our spiritual home. It is
a spark from that hearth which the communities want to keep
at home for you. It is a source of peace, of patience and of joy,
it is like a magnet which attracts all the resources of discipline
to its poles; it is like a pure, deep water in which the heaven,
with its clouds and its sun, is clearly reflected; but it also
serves the Highest in showing him a place of discipline and of
quietness, of saving order and peace. Have we not all a desire
for such a gift, unacknowledged perhaps, but still profound?
Could it not again be a healing power for us, leading to
recovery? For several reasons I think it best if we keep to the
old Epistles for meditation for the moment. God bless us in
these hours.

Today, on the first of March, warm spring sunshine has
returned for the first time; the snow is dripping from the roofs,
the air is clear, and the earth is appearing again. Our thoughts
are with those of you who in the past months have had
unimaginable experiences at the front, in winter, with the wish
that the sun and warmth and earth may soon delight you

again. 'He gives snow, he scatters hoar frost, he casts forth ice; who can stand before his cold? He sends forth his word, and melts them; he makes his wind blow, and the waters flow.' One day he will also shatter the winter and the night of the evil one and make a spring of grace and joy appear. 'The summer is near at the gate, the winter is past, the pretty flowers appear; he who has begun that will also bring it to a consummation' (Luther).

In the confidence and fellowship of this faith I commend you to God and our Lord Jesus Christ. G.S.II pp. 583-5

2. Peace-Feelers

Bonhoeffer continued his theological work, but the 'conspiracy' gained in his attention. He attached himself to the Kreisau circle and became friendly with Helmut von Moltke. Although Bonhoeffer is not listed as one of the regular members of this group, he was sympathetic to their aims. They took no part in trying to overthrow the Nazi régime, but simply prepared for the rebuilding of Germany on sound Christian lines after the inevitable fall of the Third Reich. The group usually met in Munich or Fulda, but on three occasions it came together at von Moltke's estate in Kreisau. The first of these important meetings was at Whitsun 1942, after the return of Bonhoeffer and von Moltke from Scandinavia. Their common interest at this time was their concern for Jews and their plans for a system that could be offered to the Allies after the war for a just settlement, an alternative to unconditional surrender. Von Moltke had intervened to stop drastic measures against Danish Jews and saved the life of the Norwegian Bishop Berggrav. The Resistance had had a very serious setback at the end of 1941 when Hitler dismissed Brauchitsch and became commander-in-chief of the German army himself. Bonhoeffer had always referred to the war with the code name of 'Uncle Rudy', and on his way back from Oslo he wrote to relatives in England:

17th April, 1942

BONHOEFFER TO THE LEIBHOLZ FAMILY: I went to see friends of mine up there [in Oslo] and in spite of all difficulties, I had a very satisfactory time . . . I am travelling a good deal, besides I am writing a book . . . When I wrote to you last [in September 1941, from Zürich], I thought Uncle Rudy would not live much longer, but in January and February he recovered a little, though I am quite convinced only for a very short time. He is so weak that I and my people do not believe that he can live longer than a few more months . . .

Eberhard Bethge in his biography, Dietrich Bonhoeffer, *pp. 656–9, tells the story of this Norwegian journey clearly, but there are few documents to quote. He shows that Bonhoeffer was fully committed to the conspiracy. On his third Swiss journey, 11th–23rd May, 1942, Bonhoeffer wrote a similar letter to England:*

Zürich, 13th May, 1942

BONHOEFFER TO THE LEIBHOLZ FAMILY: Uncle Rudy has recovered a little bit, but he is so terribly nervous and full of anxieties with regard to his personal future . . . his illness is so grave that I believe he will not do much longer.

Bonhoeffer was still very much concerned with 'Operation 7'. The visit to Geneva was confusing. Bonhoeffer did not meet the people he had intended to meet and he was particularly disappointed to miss Bishop Bell. He recovered from his disappointment and decided to try to meet Bell in Sweden. He wrote to Bishop Bell from Zürich on 23rd May:

BONHOEFFER TO CHICHESTER: Let me please thank you for your kind letter which I received only now . . . Mrs Martin [Niemöller] has been ill for a few weeks, so we have no news about her husband. But last time I heard from him he was said to be well physically and mentally. Since I know that Wednesday is your special day for intercessions I will meet you in prayers and my friends when I tell it will do the same. Thank you so much for letting me know that. It means so much to us. As far as I can see the day is not so far when we might meet

again not only in spirit. What a comfort to know that you will
be there in that moment! May God give us strength for the
days that will come . . .

*Bonhoeffer cut short his Swiss visit with the intention of discussing
with his friends in Berlin the daring idea of making a quick visit to
Sweden to meet with the bishop there. In Geneva, Bonhoeffer had
learned that Bell's visit to Sweden was to end officially on 2nd June.
So the plan for his journey was prepared, after discussion and various
technicalities, in three days in Berlin. Bonhoeffer flew on Saturday,
30th May, 1942, to Stockholm from Berlin. He was now a fully
fledged conspirator and he carried peace-feelers. Apparently Schönfeld
was on a similar visit, unknown to Bonhoeffer. The riddle of the two
messengers remains unsolved to this day!*

*The visit to Stockholm to meet Bishop Bell is best told in the words
of the official memorandum prepared by the bishop:*

Stockholm, 1942

Secret

MEMORANDUM OF CONVERSATION

I.

Two German pastors came from Berlin to see the Bishop of
Chichester in Stockholm at the end of May, 1942. They
arrived independently, one of them only staying 48 hours.
The bishop saw them both individually and together on four
separate days. They are men very well known to the bishop,
and have collaborated with him for many years in connection
with the ecumenical movement, the World Council of
Churches, and in different stages of the German Church
Struggle. One lives in Switzerland, but pays constant visits to
Germany. The other lives in Berlin, and is one of the leaders

of the Confessional Church; he has been forbidden by the Gestapo to preach or speak. Their purpose was:

A. To give information as to the strong, organized opposition movement inside Germany, which is making plans for the destruction of the whole Hitler régime (including Himmler, Göring, Goebbels, and the central leaders of the Gestapo, the SS and the SA), and for the setting up of a new government in Germany of

1. Representatives of certain strong anti-Nazi forces in the army and central state administration.
2. Former trade-union leaders.
3. Representatives of the Protestant and Catholic Churches, pledged to the following policy:
a) Renunciation of aggression.
b) Immediate repeal of Nuremberg laws, and co-operation in international settlement of Jewish problem.
c) Withdrawal by stages of the German forces from occupied and invaded countries.
d) Withdrawal of support to Japan, and assistance of Allies in order to end the war in the Far East.
e) Co-operation with the Allies in the rebuilding of areas destroyed or damaged by the war.

B. To ask whether the Allies, on the assumption that the whole Hitler régime had been destroyed, would be willing to negotiate with such a new German government for a peace settlement, which would provide for:

1. The setting up of a system of law and social justice inside Germany, combined with a large degree of devolution in the different main provinces.
2. The establishment of economic interdependence between the different nations of Europe, both as just in itself, and as the strongest possible guarantee against militarism.
3. The establishment of a representative federation of free

nations or states, including a free Polish and a free Czech nation.

4. The establishment of a European army for the control of Europe, of which the German army could form a part, under central authority.

II. *Character of the opposition*

The opposition has been developing for some time, and had some existence before the war. The war gives it its chance, which it is now waiting to seize. The opposition crystallized in the autumn of 1941, and might have seized an opportunity in December, 1941, with the refusal of many officers to go on fighting in Russia. But no lead was given. Hitler's last speech, openly claiming to be above all laws, showed the German people more and more clearly the complete anarchy of the régime. The opposition has full confidence in the strength of the German army, and is ready to go on with the war to the bitter end if the Allies were to refuse to treat with a new government controlling a non-Hitlerite Germany, after the overthrow of the whole Hitler régime; but it believes that to continue the war on the present or on a greater scale in such circumstances would be to condemn millions more to destruction, especially in the occupied countries.

It also believes that a fight to the finish would be suicidal for Europe. Hence its desire first to destroy Hitler and his régime, and then to reach a peace settlement in which all the nations of Europe shall be economically interdependent, shall be protected against aggression by the possession of an adequate European military force, and shall be in some way federated. The opposition, while having some hesitations with regard to Soviet Russia, has the hope (as a result of impressions made by some of the high Russian officers on some of the German officers) of the possibility of reaching an understanding.

III. *Organization of the opposition*

The opposition is based on members of the state administration, the state police, former trade-union chiefs, and high officers in the army. It has an organization in every Ministry, military officers in all the big towns, generals in command or holding high office in key places very near the generals. It has key men armed in the broadcasting centres, in the big factories, and in the main centres of war and gas supply services. It is impossible to tell the numbers of the opposition. The point is that key positions everywhere are held by members of the opposition, and that key positions in Germany itself are of chief importance.

The following names were given as those of men who were deeply involved in the opposition movement:

Generaloberst Beck . . . Chief of General Staff before the Czecho-Slovak crisis in 1938. Aged 60.

Generaloberst von Hammerstein . . . Chief of General Staff before Beck.

Goerdeler . . . Ex-price commissar, former Lord Mayor of Leipzig. Civil front leader.

Leuschner . . . Former president of the united trade unions.

Kaiser . . . Catholic trade union leader.

All the above are said to be strong Christian characters, and the most important of all are Beck and Goerdeler.

Certain other persons of a less clear Christian character would be available, such as Schacht. Most of the field-marshals are reliable, especially von Kluge, von Bock, Kuchler, and possibly Witzleben. Whether a member of the opposition or not, was not stated, but the question was asked whether England would favour a monarchy in Germany, in which case Prince Louis Ferdinand was possible. He had been fetched from the United States by Hitler after the heroic death of the crown prince's eldest son. He had been working in a Ford factory as a workman, and now lives on a farm in East Prussia. He is a Christian, has outspoken social interests, and is known to one of the two German pastors. The leaders of the Protestant and Catholic Churches are also closely in touch with the whole opposition movement, particularly Bishop Wurm of Württemberg (Protestant) and Bishop von Preysing of Berlin, acting as spokesman of the Catholic bishops. (At the same time it should be said that included in the opposition are many who are not only filled with deep penitence for the crimes committed in Germany's name, but even say, 'Christians do not wish to escape repentance, or chaos, if it is God's will to bring it upon me'.)

IV. *Action of the opposition*
The opposition is aware of impending revolt inside the Nazi party, of Himmler and his followers against Hitler; but while a successful *coup* by Himmler might be of service to the opposition, the complete elimination of Hitler and Himmler and the whole régime is indispensable. The plan of the opposition is the achievement of a purge as nearly simultaneous as possible on the home front and in the occupied countries, after which a new government would be set up. In the securing of a new government, the opposition realizes the need of an effective police control throughout Germany and the occupied and invaded territories; and it appeared that the help of the Allied armies as assistants in the maintenance of order would be both necessary and welcome, all the more if it were possible to associate with the Allied armies the army of a neutral power in the maintenance of order.

V. *Enquiries by the opposition of the Allied governments*
The above being the policy and plan of the opposition, the

question arises as to what encouragement can be given to its leaders with a view to setting the whole process in motion and the facing of all the dangers involved. As examples of encouragement, such enquiries as the following are made:

1. Would the Allied governments be willing to treat with a new bona fide German government, set up on the lines described in A of Section I above, for a peace of the character described in B of Section I above? (The answer to this might be *privately* given to a representative of the opposition through a neutral country.)

2. Could the Allies announce now publicly to the world in the clearest terms that, once Hitler and the whole régime were overthrown, they would be prepared to negotiate with a new German government which renounced aggression and was pledged to a policy of the character described in A of Section I above, with a view to a peace settlement of the character described in B of Section I above?

VI. *Means of communication*

Arrangements have been made by which any reaction in important British quarters which the Bishop of Chichester might be able to obtain could be communicated through a neutral channel. The British Minister in Stockholm was fully informed at the time of the tenor of the conversations. On his advice the bishop warned the two German pastors not only that the American and Russian and the other Allied governments would necessarily be concerned, but that the Foreign Office might take the view that the situation was too uncertain to justify any expression of opinion on its part. On the other hand, if it were thought desirable to obtain further elucidation, a confidential meeting could be arranged at Stockholm between a German representative and a representative of the Foreign Office or other suitable person.   G.S.I pp. 372–7

A statement by Schönfeld, carried back to England by Bishop Bell, explains the situation in Germany:

STATEMENT BY A GERMAN PASTOR AT
STOCKHOLM, 31st May, 1942

I

The many opposition circles in Germany who had beforehand no real contact with each other have crystallized during the last winter into active opposition groups working now closely together as centres of a strong opposition movement to the whole Nazi régime on the European continent.

There are three main groups of action preparing definitely to overthrow the Nazi régime and to bring about a complete change of power.

1. Essential parts of the leadership in the army and in the central state administration. (In the army they include key men in the highest command (OKW) for the front troops, navy and air forces, as well as in the central command of the home military forces; also in the state administration the liaison men to the state police forces largely in opposition to the Gestapo.)

2. The leaders of the former trade unions and other active liaison men to large parts of the workers. (Through a network of key men systematically developed during the last six months they control now key positions in the main industrial centres as well as in the big cities like Berlin, Hamburg, Cologne, and throughout the whole country.)

3. The leaders of the Evangelical Churches (under Bishop Wurm) and of the Roman Catholic Church (the Fulda bishops' conference) acting together as the great corporations and as centres of resistance and reconstruction.

By their close co-operation these three key groups of action have formed the strong opposition movement which, in the given situation, would have sufficient power to overthrow the present régime because of their control over large masses now having arms in their hands, and, as regards the workers, at their disposal.

II

The leaders of these key groups are now prepared to take the next chance for the elimination of Hitler, Himmler, Göring, Goebbels, Ley, and co., together with whom the central leaders of the Gestapo, the SS and the SA would be destroyed at the same time, especially also in the occupied countries. This change of power would not lead to the establishment of a military clique controlling the whole situation but to the coming into power of a government composed by strong representatives of the three key groups who are able and definitely prepared to bring about a complete change of the present system of lawlessness and social injustice.

Their programme is determined by the following main aims:

1. A German nation governed by law and social justice with a large degree of responsible self-administration through the different main provinces.

2. Reconstruction of the economic order according to truly socialistic lines; instead of self-sufficient autarchy a close co-operation between free nations, their economic interdependence becoming the strongest possible guarantee against self-reactionary European militarism.

3. A European federation of free states or nations, including Great Britain, which would co-operate in a close way with other federations of nations. This federation of free European nations, to which would belong a free Polish and a free Czech nation, should have a common executive, under the authority

of which a European army should be created for the permanent ordering of European security.

The foundations and principles of national and social life within this federation of free European nations should be orientated or re-orientated towards the fundamental principles of Christian faith and life.

III

The internal circumstances are becoming now peculiarly favourable to a *coup d'état* by the army and the other combined forces of the opposition. It would help and quicken this process towards the change of power along the lines mentioned above (see II) if the Allies would make it clear whether they are prepared for a European peace settlement along the lines indicated.

If otherwise the Allies insist on a fight to the finish, the German opposition, with the German army, is ready to go on with the war to the bitter end in spite of its wish to end the Nazi régime.

In the case of agreement for a European peace settlement as indicated, the opposition government would, after a *coup d'état*, withdraw gradually all its forces from the occupied and invaded countries.

It would announce at once that it would restitute the Jewish part of the population at once to a decent status, give back the stolen property, and co-operate with all other nations for a comprehensive solution of the Jewish problem.

It would be prepared to take its full share in the common efforts for the rebuilding of the areas destroyed or damaged by the war. It would declare itself at once disinterested in any further co-operation with the Japanese government and its war aims, being prepared, on the contrary, to place at disposal its forces and war material for finishing the war in the Far East.

It would be prepared to co-operate for a real solution of the colonial problem along the lines of a true mandate system in which all member nations of the European federation should participate, together with the other nations or federations of nations concerned.

It is to be expected that representatives of the SS will offer the elimination of Hitler in order to secure for themselves power and a negotiated peace. It would be a real support for the start of the whole process towards the change of power as indicated if they would be encouraged in any way to go on. It would help the opposition leaders to mobilize and to lead all the other forces of the army and the nation against Himmler and the SS leaders, against whom the bitterness and hatred is greater than against anyone else.

In regard to the Russian problem

1. The opposition groups have no aims to conquer or to get for Germany parts of Russia as a colonial area.

2. They hope it may be in the future possible to co-operate in a really peaceful way with Russia, especially in the economic and cultural field.

3. But they are not convinced that the totalitarian methods of revolutionary brutal warfare would be changed without very effective guarantees, even when the totalitarian régime in Central Europe would have been abolished.

4. They would regard the building up of an Orthodox Russian Church by the renewal of Christian faith in Russia as a real common basis which could further more than anything else the co-operation between Russia and the European federation.

G.S.I. pp. 378–81

Before leaving Stockholm, Bonhoeffer wrote a letter of thanks to Bell:

179

1st June, 1942

BONHOEFFER TO CHICHESTER: Let me express my deep and sincere gratitude for the hours you have spent with me. It still seems to me like a dream to have seen you, to have spoken to you, to have heard your voice. I think these days will remain in my memory as some of the greatest of my life. This spirit of fellowship and of Christian brotherliness will carry me through the darkest hour, and even if things go worse than we hope and expect, the light of these few days will never extinguish in my heart. These impressions of these days were so overwhelming that I cannot express them in words. I feel ashamed when I think of all your goodness and at the same time I feel full of hope for the future.

God be with you on your way home, in your work and always. I shall think of you on Wednesday. Please pray for us. We need it.   G.S.I p. 382

What followed is now history and can be told by the correspondence which passed between the bishop and Anthony Eden, then British Foreign Secretary.

The Bishop's Lodging, 22 The Droveway, Hove,
18th June, 1942

CHICHESTER TO EDEN: I have just got back from Sweden with what seems to me very important confidential information about proposals from a big opposition movement in Germany. Two German pastors, both of them well known to me for twelve years or more (one of them an intimate friend), came expressly from Berlin to see me at Stockholm. The movement is backed by leaders of both the Protestant and Catholic Churches. They gave me pretty full particulars, and names of leading persons in the civil administration, in the labour movement and in the army, who are involved. The credentials of these pastors are such that I am convinced of their integrity and the risks they have run.

I ought to say that I was staying at the British Legation, and told Mr Mallet all about it. He thought the matter important enough to justify me in asking if I might see you and tell you personally what the pastors had told me. The information is a sequel to the memorandum you have already seen, brought from Geneva by Visser 't Hooft of the World Council of Churches, and having to do with von Trott.

I have also today reported to Mr Warner on my visit to Sweden and given him some information as to the visit of the pastors. It is on his suggestion that I am writing direct to you, and I should be very grateful if you could receive me. I will bring my papers with me. I could come any time on Saturday, or from 3 p.m. onwards on Monday. From Tuesday to Friday I have some engagements which I cannot break in my diocese. I do not know whether you will be at West Dean this weekend. If so, and it suited you, I could easily come over after tea on the Sunday.

Personal and Private   *Foreign Office, S.W.1, 17th July, 1942*
EDEN TO CHICHESTER: When you came to see me on June 30th, you were good enough to leave with me a memorandum of your conversations with two German pastors whom you met in Stockholm at the end of May, together with the record of a statement by one of the pastors.

These interesting documents have now been given the most careful examination, and, without casting any reflection on the bona fides of your informants, I am satisfied that it would not be in the national interest for any reply whatever to be sent to them. I realize that this decision may cause you some disappointment, but in view of the delicacy of the issues involved I feel that I must ask you to accept it, and I am sure that you will understand.

25th July, 1942

CHICHESTER TO EDEN: Many thanks for your letter of the 17th July. I am very glad that after most careful examination of the documents which I left with you, you feel that no reflection can be cast on the bona fides of the two German pastors. I must of course bow to your decision that it is not in the national interest to make any reply to them personally. But I do greatly hope that it may be possible for you in the near future to make it plain in an emphatic and public way that the British government (and the Allies) have no desire to enslave a Germany which has rid itself of Hitler and Himmler and their accomplices. I found much evidence on many sides in Sweden, in addition to my information from the two pastors, of the existence of a sharp distinction between the Nazis as such and a very large body of other Germans. It is the drawing of this distinction (with its consequences) by the Government in the most emphatic way which is so anxiously awaited by the opposition.

I have read your Nottingham speech with great attention and with much sympathy. I appreciate all you say about our resolution to continue to fight against the dictator powers until they are all finally disarmed and rendered powerless to do further injury to mankind. I appreciate to the full your words about the recent atrocities, and your statement that these atrocities represent the policy of the German government, and your declaration of a resolve to exact full and stern retribution. All these words are clearly intended to show the consequence of the determined British and Allied policy to have no truck with the Nazis. But if you could at some convenient opportunity make it plain that the infliction of stern retribution is not intended for those in Germany who are against the German government, who repudiate the Nazi system and are filled with shame by the Nazi crimes, it would, I am sure, have a powerful and encouraging effect on the spirit of the opposition. I cannot get out of my mind the words which the Norwegian Minister used in a private conversation with me in Stockholm about the reality of the German opposition. The opposition, he said, hates Hitler but sees no hope held out by the Allies of any better treatment for the anti-Nazis than for the Nazis. 'It is either this (i.e. Hitler) or slavery. We hate this, but we prefer it to slavery.' And I see that Goebbels has just been intensifying his propaganda in the German home front to the effect that the Allies are determined to destroy Germany. I do not believe that Lord Vansittart's policy is the policy of the British government. But so long as the British government fails to repudiate it, or make it clear that those who are opposed to Hitler and Himmler will receive better treatment at our hands than Hitler and Himmler and their accomplices, it is not unnatural that the opposition in Germany should believe that the Vansittart policy holds the field.

Mr Churchill said in his first speech as Prime Minister in the House of Commons on May 13th, 1940, that our policy was 'to wage war against a monstrous tyranny never surpassed in the dark and lamentable catalogue of human crime', and that our aim was 'victory at all costs'. If there are men in Germany also ready to wage war against the monstrous tyranny of the Nazis from within, is it right to discourage or ignore them? Can we afford to reject their aid in achieving our end? If we by our silence allow them to believe that there is no hope for any Germany, whether Hitlerite or anti-Hitlerite, that is what in effect we are doing.

Confidential   *Foreign Office, S.W.1, 4th August, 1942*
EDEN TO CHICHESTER: Thank you very much for your letter of July 25th about the German problem. I am very conscious of the importance of what you say about not dis-

couraging any elements of opposition in Germany to the Nazi régime. You will remember that in my speech at Edinburgh on May 8th I devoted quite a long passage to Germany and concluded by saying that if any section of the German people really wished to see a return to a German state based on respect for law and the rights of the individual, they must understand that no one would believe them until they had taken active steps to rid themselves of their present régime.

For the present I do not think that it would be advisable for me to go any further in a public statement. I realize the dangers and difficulties to which the opposition in Germany is exposed, but they have so far given little evidence of their existence and until they show that they are willing to follow the example of the oppressed peoples of Europe in running risks and taking active steps to oppose and overthrow the Nazi rule of terror I do not see how we can usefully expand the statements which have already been made by members of the Government about Germany. I think these statements have made it quite clear that we do not intend to deny to Germany a place in the future Europe, but that the longer the German people tolerate the Nazi régime the greater becomes their responsibility for the crimes which that régime is committing in their name.

As from: The Bishop's Lodging, 22 The Droveway, Hove,
Private   *17th August, 1942*
CHICHESTER TO EDEN: Very many thanks for your letter of August 4th about the German problem, which has been forwarded to me in Scotland.

I much appreciate what you say about your consciousness of the importance of not discouraging any elements of opposition in Germany to the Nazi régime, and your reference to the very important speech which you made in Edinburgh on May 8.

I also see the force of your point that the opposition in Germany should be ready to take similar risks to those taken by the oppressed peoples in Europe. The German opposition would probably reply that there is a difference, in view of the fact that the oppressed peoples have been promised deliverance by the Allies, and that Germany has not exactly been promised that. At the same time I fully see the point has got to be rubbed home that the opposition Germans themselves must do their part in opposing and overthrowing the Nazi rule.

Certainly the pastors and their friends in Germany are fully alive to the grave character of the responsibility borne by the German people for the crimes committed by the Nazis in their name. The hopes of a return to a German state based on respect for law and the rights of the individual, after the overthrow of the Nazis, and of a place for a reformed Germany in the future Europe, ought to be powerful factors in making the opposition declare itself more and more plainly. G.S.I pp. 383–8

It was obvious that the 'final solution of the Jewish problem' had so blackened Germany in the eyes of the world that no one felt able to trust her or treat her as human. Churchill's great war effort depended upon a complete victory and he was in no mood to listen to half-measures. It was 'unconditional surrender' or nothing. A sad letter from an anxious Bonhoeffer, written on a subsequent visit to Switzerland, completes the story, as told by this correspondence.

28th August, 1942

BONHOEFFER TO CHICHESTER: I have just received a letter from my sister in which she tells me that she has met you after your long journey. I am so glad to know that you have returned safely and that you have already seen my people. Since I wrote you last not much has changed here. Things are going as I expected them to go. But the length of time is, of course, sometimes a little enervating. Still I am hopeful that the day might not be too far when the bad dream will be over and we shall meet again. The task before us will then be greater than ever before. But I hope we shall be prepared for it. I should be glad to hear from you soon. Wednesday has for many of my friends become the special day for ecumenical intercession. Martin [Niemöller] and the other friends send you all their love and thanks. Would you be good enough to give my love to my sister's family?   G.S.I p. 389

For Bonhoeffer there was a life to be lived in Nazi Germany and ultimately a death to die. His 'peace-feelers' had failed. He continued to live dangerously. The small group of seven Jews arrived safely in Switzerland and Bonhoeffer could feel content that at least 'Operation 7' had been a success. It was however to prove fatal for him. He was now very much under suspicion, as was the Abwehr *and Admiral Canaris. In that same month of September, Bonhoeffer's application for a permit to visit the Balkans and Switzerland was turned down. Events were moving rapidly. The entry of America into the war had changed the balance considerably and by 8th November the Allies had landed in North Africa. Bonhoeffer's 'peace-feelers' and his foreign travel were over. He began to consider a private life, and on 24th November he went to Pätzig to discuss his engagement to Maria von Wedemeyer with her mother. It was to be a tragically curtailed engagement, but Bonhoeffer went through the proper procedure required of his class. He was, in fact, never once alone with his fiancée and the engagement eventually took place almost on the eve of his arrest. Meanwhile, he turned his attention to his former students and wrote two letters of comfort to them in 1942.*

The first is undated, but deals with the controversial business of legalization. Young pastors of the Confessing Church had not registered with the state Church and therefore could not be legally assigned to a 'living'. The debate continued on whether it was better to become legalized and thereby exercise a strong influence on the

*official Church or to refuse legalization and maintain a continuing
protest. Bonhoeffer made his point of view quite clear:*

1942

Let me answer the letters about the question of legalization, all
together. One person writes as one who has just been legalized,
the second as one who has just rejected legalization, the third
is engaged in thinking it over. The questions are all the same. I
want to try to clarify some things in principle.

   1. In times of uncertainty the following rules hold for us:

a) I should never make a decision in uncertainty; the *status quo*
has precedence over change, unless I recognize the need for
change with certainty.

b) I should never act alone, firstly because I need the advice of
the brothers, secondly because the brothers need me, and
thirdly because there is a church discipline which I must not
treat lightly.

c) I should never make a hasty decision or allow it to be forced
on me. If one door closes for me today, God will open
another one when he wills to.

From this rule it follows that our present war situation is a
particularly inappropriate time for undertaking a far-reaching
alteration of the Church's course. I must wait more than ever
for the word of my church government, and be patient. Any
decision which gives the brothers at home a more advantageous
position than those at the front is even more questionable.

   2. The question of proper training for the preacher of the
gospel is worth risking everything for. Readiness to leave the
ordained ministry, even to refrain from any exercising of
spiritual office and to serve Christ in another calling rather
than to subject oneself to a false spiritual authority (for this is
what it is) remains a legitimate evangelical position. It is
doubtful whether the highest price, whether such renunciation

must be demanded from every individual where all attempts at proper training have been made impossible in practice and through the law, in other words, where martyrdom is the necessary consequence of any such attempt. Still, at the moment that is by no means certain, as even the reason for the judgement at the trial has not yet been given. Readiness to enter the ministry without allegiance to any church government (for a recognition of the false church government is impossible), 'preserving one's personal theological convictions', to serve as a pastor, can under the present circumstances no longer be rejected *in principle* as a Christian possibility, but it is set about with heavy dangers and responsibilities for the Church and the individual. That must be seen.

3. What does the directness of the Church's way mean? Can what was true in the Synod of Dahlem now be false? Is our conscience bound to Dahlem? Only God's word makes our way direct, even if to our eyes it is crooked. Only God's word is true. Our certainty is bound to God's word alone . . . (*Letter incomplete.*)   G.S.II pp. 594–5

His circular letter, telling of recent casualties went out about the time that he was discussing his forthcoming engagement to Maria von Wedemeyer:

29th November, Advent 1, 1942

BONHOEFFER TO THE BRETHREN: At the head of a letter which is intended to summon you to joy at a serious hour must stand the names of the brothers who have been killed since last I wrote to you: P. Walde, W. Brandenburg, Hermann Schroder, R. Lynker, Erwin Schutz, K. Rhode, Alfred Viol, Kurt Onnasch, Fritz's second brother, and in addition to them, many of whom are well known to you, Major von Wedemeyer and his oldest son Max, my former pupil for confirmation.

'With everlasting joy upon their heads . . .' (Isa. 35. 10).
We do not grudge it them; indeed, should we say that sometimes we envy them in the stillness? Since ancient times,
accidie – sorrowfulness of the heart, 'resignation' – has been
one of the deadly sins. 'Serve the Lord with gladness' (Ps.
100. 2) summons us to the Scriptures. This is what our life has
been given to us for, what it has been preserved for up till now.
Joy belongs, not only to those who have been called home,
but also to the living, and no one shall take it from us. We are
one with them in this joy, but never in sorrow. How shall we
be able to help those who have become joyless and fearful
unless we ourselves are supported by courage and joy? I don't
mean by this something fabricated, compelled, but something
given, free. Joy dwells with God; it descends from him and
seizes spirit, soul and body, and where this joy has grasped a
man it grows greater, carries him away, opens closed doors.
There is a joy which knows nothing of sorrow, need and
anxiety of the heart; it has no duration, and it can only drug
one for the moment. The joy of God has been through the
poverty of the crib and the distress of the cross; therefore it is
insuperable, irrefutable. It does not deny the distress where it is,
but finds God in the midst of it, indeed precisely there; it does
not contest the most grievous sin, but finds forgiveness in just
this way; it looks death in the face, yet finds life in death itself.
We are concerned with this joy which has overcome. It alone
is worth believing, it alone helps and heals. The joy of our
friends who have been called home is also the joy of those who
have overcome – the risen one bears the marks of the cross
upon his body; we are still engaged in conflict daily, they have
overcome for all time. God alone knows how near to us or far
from us stands the last overcoming, in which our own death
can become joy. 'With peace and joy I go hence . . .'

Some of us suffer a great deal from having our senses dulled in the face of all the sorrows which these war years have brought with them. Someone said to me recently: 'I pray every day for my senses not to become dulled.' That is certainly a good prayer. And yet we must be careful not to confuse ourselves with Christ. Christ endured all suffering and all human guilt to the full, indeed he was Christ in that he suffered everything alone. But Christ could suffer alongside men because at the same time he was able to redeem them from suffering. He had his power to suffer with men from his love and his power to redeem men. We are not called to burden ourselves with the sorrows of the whole world; in the end, we cannot suffer with men in our own strength because we are unable to redeem. A suppressed desire to suffer with man in one's own strength must become resignation. We are simply called to look with utter joy on the one who really suffered with men and became their redeemer. We may joyfully believe that there was, there is, a man to whom no human sorrow and no human sin is strange and who in the profoundest love achieved our redemption. Only in such joy towards Christ, the Redeemer, are we saved from having our senses dulled by the pressure of human sorrow, or from becoming resigned under the experience of suffering. We believe in Christ only as much as . . . in Christ . . . (*Letter incomplete.*)   G.S.II pp. 596–8

That letter about joy in the midst of sorrows was a fitting end to the year that had been his fullest year as 'double agent'. 1943 opened with the ominous declaration of 'unconditional surrender' as the only possible peace terms (Casablanca, 14th January). That was the end of all 'peace-feelers'. A few days later, Bonhoeffer was engaged to Maria von Wedemeyer. It was a year of many abortive attempts to assassinate Hitler, but Bonhoeffer was not involved. The last family celebration he was able to take part in was his father's seventy-fifth

birthday on 31st March, when the Führer himself sent a greeting:
HITLER TO KARL BONHOEFFER: In the name of the German people I bestow on Professor Emeritus Dr Karl Bonhoeffer the Goethe medal for art and science, instituted by the late Reich President Hindenburg.

A few days later, on 5th April, 1943, Dietrich was arrested. Here is Bethge's account of the arrest:

At midday on Monday, 5th April, Bonhoeffer tried to ring up his sister Christine von Dohnanyi at her Sakrow house, from the Marienburger Allee. But his call was answered by an unknown man's voice. He at once thought: The house is being searched! Without disturbing his parents, he went across to his sister Ursula Schleicher in the next-door house, and got her to give him a good meal, after which he went up to his attic to check the contents of his desk once more. Then he waited next door with the Schleichers and me. About four o'clock his father came across: 'There are two men wanting to speak to you upstairs in your room!' Shortly afterwards, Judge Advocate Roeder and the Gestapo official Sonderegger drove off with him.

That was the third arrest that Roeder and Sonderegger made in person that day, and the fifth that was made on their orders. The others concerned Dohnanyi and Josef Müller and their wives. *Dietrich Bonhoeffer* pp. 690–1

PART THREE

The Prisoner

1943 *5th April* – House-search and arrest, taken to Tegel prison.

29th April – Warrant for Bonhoeffer's arrest drawn up, charged with 'subversion of the armed forces'.

16th September – Dr Wergin confirmed as defence lawyer for Bonhoeffer.

25th September – Charged with anti-war activity.

18th November – First of his letters to Eberhard Bethge, 'Letters to a Friend' (*Letters and Papers from Prison*).

First Christmas in prison.

1944 *January* – Chief interrogator dismissed.

February – Canaris dismissed from the *Abwehr*, now incorporated into the Reich Security Head Office.

6th March – First heavy daylight air-raid on Tegel prison.

30th April – First 'theological' letter from prison.

May – Charge against Bonhoeffer indefinitely postponed.

20th July – Von Stauffenberg's attempt on Hitler's life.

22nd September – Gestapo Commissar Sonderegger discovers files in the *Abwehr* air-raid shelter at Zossen.

5th October – Escape plan abandoned because of arrest of Dietrich's brother Klaus, his brother-in-law, Rüdiger Schleicher, and Perels – fear of reprisals if he escaped.

8th October – Moved to Gestapo cellars in the Prinz-Albrecht-Strasse.

1945 *February* – In Buchenwald concentration camp.

3rd April – Removed from Buchenwald to Regensburg.

5th April – Annihilation order announced at Hitler's midday conference.

6th April – Moved to Schönberg in the Bavarian woods.

8th April – Moved to Flossenbürg during the night, summary court martial.

9th April – Executed together with Oster, Sack, Canaris, Strünck and Gehre; von Dohnanyi killed in Sachsenhausen.

23rd April – Klaus Bonhoeffer, Rüdiger Schleicher and F. J. Perels killed in Berlin.

25th April – Eberhard Bethge escaped from prison in Berlin.

30th April – Adolf Hitler ended his life.

1. On Trial

On Monday, 5th April, 1943, Bonhoeffer was taken to Tegel prison and spent his first night in the cell there on the 6th. There is a description of that first night given by Eberhard Bethge in his biography:

The night of 6th April, 1943, was cold in the reception cell at Tegel. Bonhoeffer could not bring himself to use the blankets of the plank-bed, as he could not stand the stench that rose from them. There was someone crying loudly in the next cell. In the morning, dry bread was thrown through a crack in the door. The staff had been instructed not to speak to the new arrival. The warder called him a 'blackguard' ('*Strolch*').

Bonhoeffer was then taken to the section where the solitary confinement cells were, where those condemned to death were held, bound hand and foot. A few days later he too was hand-cuffed when he was taken to town for his first interrogation at the Reich War Court (*Reichskriegsgericht*). As a member of the *Abwehr* he came under the jurisdiction of a military court, but Colonel Roeder, who conducted the hearing, always had beside him officials from the Reich Security Head Office (*Reichssicherheitshauptamt*).

The old Tegel prison was one of the military interrogation prisons. At first, Bonhoeffer was housed on the third floor, but later in the single cell, No. 92, on the first, because of the increased danger of bombing attacks. He spent eighteen months in Tegel, until, on 8th October, 1944, he was transferred to the detention cellar on Prinz-Albrecht-Strasse, the house prison of the Reich Security Head Office, close to the Anhalter railway station. *Dietrich Bonhoeffer* p. 703

The period of eighteen months which he spent in the Tegel cell is divided into three parts:
a) April–July, 1943 – *interrogation by Roeder, ending with a charge being laid against him.*
b) August 1943–April 1944 – *continually rising hopes that there would be a trial.*
c) April–September, 1944 – *Bonhoeffer accepts the strategy of 'letting the case ride'.*

Everything was changed by the discovery of documents at Zossen in the Abwehr *air-raid shelter on 22nd September, 1944. After this, Bonhoeffer was moved to Prinz-Albrecht-Strasse and suffered at the hands of the Gestapo for the rest of his life. Until that time, he had been a reasonably free prisoner with the facility to communicate which he used richly. These eighteen months of relative freedom must be examined first:*

A] UNTIL JULY 1943

At first he concentrated on his case and struggled to face his trial and prove his innocence. The first letter we have from prison was to his parents and it assured them of his safety and his power to adapt himself to the unpleasant conditions of prison life. He recalled with pleasure the family celebrations which had taken place on the occasion of his father's seventy-fifth birthday only a few days before he was arrested.

During this period all Bonhoeffer's letters had to pass through the censor and were read by Roeder who was his judicial interrogator. Those who read those letters as they now appear in Letters and Papers from Prison *will however be less impressed by the influence*

*of the censor than by the deep concern of Bonhoeffer that his parents
should not worry unduly about him. He kept in constant touch with
the ordinary events of the household.*

*Yet there seems little doubt that the experience of prison deeply
affected him from the beginning. It was probably during this first
period that he wrote some fragments of a drama. In these pieces he
depicted a man who had faced death and from that time onwards
saw everything differently. If Bonhoeffer had been released from
prison in July 1943 the experience would still have been profound.
We can see this from the drama fragments:*

PASSAGES FROM A DRAMA FRAGMENT (1943)

I

From Scene 1. Christoph to his father:

. . . Anyway, it was a spirited evening again. After the incident,
someone began to talk about the right of free speech and before
long we were back again in the middle of the debate about the
freedom of the citizen. Things warmed up. Father, I argued
that one should never make freedom a slogan for the masses,
because that led to the most dreadful slavery. Freedom was
always something to be limited to the very few, the noble, the
select. For the rest, law and order took the place of freedom.
I also said that there had to be superiors and inferiors among
men and that anyone who did not understand this fact was
introducing chaos. And finally, I even said that there were
people who were noble by nature, who were destined for rule
and for freedom, and that there were also people who were
rabble by nature, who had to serve, and that there was nothing
more fearful and more disruptive than when this order
collapsed and the rabble ruled and the nobility served. The two
groups of people were distinguished by the fact that the rabble
only knew how to live, whereas the nobility also knew how to

die ... They almost flew at my throat because of these remarks, and now next time I am to justify my statements to them ...

II

From Scene 2. His friend reads in Christoph's diary:
I am speaking to you in order to protect the great words which have been given to men from being misused. They are out of place on the lips of the mob and in the headlines of newspapers; they belong in the hearts of the few who guard and protect them with their life. It is never a good sign when what has always been the tranquil and firm possession, the responsible attitude, of all well-disposed members of society is hawked on the streets as the latest wisdom. The people who preserve true values with their life, their work and their homes turn in distaste from the eloquent words with which men want to make the rabble into prophets. What well-disposed man still utters contaminated words like freedom, brotherliness, indeed Germany? He looks for them in the tranquillity of the sanctuary which only the humble and faithful may approach. Each of us has been proud of these ideals; those who bandy them about today are those who find them profitable. Let us reverence the great ideals for a while in silence; let us learn for a time to do the right thing without words. In this way, a new nobility will develop in our time around the tranquil sanctuary of the great ideals. Neither birth nor success will be its foundation, but humility, faith and sacrifice. There is an infallible standard for the great and the small, the valid and the invalid, the true and the false, for the word that carries weight and for trivial gossip – death. Anyone who knows that his death is near is determined, but he is also silent. Without words, misunderstood and alone if need be, he does what is necessary and right, he makes his sacrifice.

What sort of great words are these? Why do I not simply say what I mean and what I know? Or if I do not want to do that, why do I not keep completely silent? How hard it is to do what is necessary and right, really without words, misunderstood . . .

III

Scene 3.

(In Heinrich's room, bed, table, stool, sofa, picture, all in the style of the cheapest rented accommodation. A pistol on the table, a bottle of schnapps and a glass, the remains of a meal, a couple of pieces of paper. Smoking a cigarette, H. paces restlessly up and down. The door opens gently, without a knock; a middle-aged man, in the inconspicuous but correct dark clothing of a middle-class businessman, comes in; he wears spectacles which make his eyes almost invisible; his face is completely expressionless, impenetrable, smooth, masklike.)

STRANGER: Good evening, young sir. *(When there is no answer . . .)* You called me.

HEINRICH: You are mistaken. I don't know you.

STRANGER: Of course you don't; that is why you called me. You want to make my acquaintance.

HEINRICH: I tell you, it's a mistake. I am not in the habit of wanting to make people's acquaintance – at least, with one exception, but you are not that.

STRANGER: Who is this interesting exception, may I ask?

HEINRICH: That's hardly your business. So perhaps you will be so good – *(Goes to the door.)*

STRANGER: As you will not tell me, perhaps I may be allowed to tell you: the interesting exception is a medical student of your own age, magnanimous, wise, idealistically inclined.

HEINRICH (*taken aback*): What do you want with me? Who are you, anyway?

STRANGER: Your neighbour, young sir, who sees you go out and come in, morning and evening, who sees the light burning in your room into the early hours, and who knows what goes on in this room in the lonely hours of the night.

HEINRICH: I don't look for conversation with my neighbours, particularly with inquisitive ones.

STRANGER: Inquisitive might be an inappropriate expression. I have no need to be inquisitive.

HEINRICH: Why do you watch me then? Why are you interested in me?

STRANGER: That, if I may say so, is my occupation.

HEINRICH: What is your occupation?

STRANGER: It can't be put in a word. Shall we say – I'm a representative.

HEINRICH (*laughs*): So, you've been spying on me! You've seen that I haven't a number of things which a person of my status needs, and you want to sell them to me. It would have been better if you'd taken a closer look at my purse. What do you sell, Persian carpets, English material, Parisian perfume, American cars . . . ?

STRANGER: You misunderstand me, sir.

HEINRICH: Or perhaps you represent life insurance?

STRANGER: Quite the opposite.

HEINRICH: That's an interesting remark. The opposite of life insurance! Would you please explain yourself? Here, have a drink. (*Both sit down.*) Tell me, what company do you represent?

STRANGER: The most widespread and influential firm on earth.

HEINRICH: And that is – ?

STRANGER: Death.

HEINRICH: Man, are you mad?

STRANGER: Please keep calm, young sir, and let me assure you that I am quite sane. If you wish, I will tell you more about it, and I am certain that you will understand me very, very well.

HEINRICH: I won't disguise the fact that under the circumstances I am very interested in your business. But you must let me ask a few questions. I am indeed interested in your business – perhaps more than you suspect.

STRANGER: I know.

HEINRICH: So the essential questions would be: How did you get this job? What are the wages? And who gives you the information?

STRANGER: Wise questions. I see we will get on well. How did I get my job? Let me first ask you a question which will make it much easier for us to understand each other. Have you ever been condemned to death?

HEINRICH (*hesitates*): No – yes.

STRANGER: No! You once thought that you had been condemned to death, when you went to war. You had condemned yourself to death. That is something quite different.

HEINRICH (*gloomily*): God had condemned me to death, but people deceived God.

STRANGER (*winces*): Humbug, nothing but humbug. You had got something into your head, you had had enough of life, you thought that you would give orders to Death. You underestimated Death. He didn't come.

HEINRICH: Death comes when I want. Here! (*Takes hold of the pistol.*)

STRANGER: You're wrong, fatally wrong, if you persist in that. You can only shoot when Death lets you. Not a moment sooner. Have you never had the thing in your hand at some time and wanted to pull the trigger – but it didn't go, you couldn't, something – you yourself didn't know what – held your index finger firm? Don't say that it was your cowardice, your desire for life. You are not a coward and you don't desire life. That was Death.

HEINRICH: Death is an event like war, storm, earthquake. These events are in the hand of God.

STRANGER (*winces again*): Wrong, utterly wrong, you must learn a great deal more, young sir. Death is not an event, it is a – being, a – lord, – the Lord. So, to make it short: I was condemned to death – incidentally, I was of course innocent; but that's irrelevant here. I looked Death in the face for four weeks. First uncomprehendingly, as on a dark night, when one seems to have an impenetrable black wall before one's eyes, then terror-struck, as though beneath a falling axe, then again with burning desire, as though for a bride on the eve of a wedding, then full of wonderment, as though faced with a powerful chief. When I was released it was too late; I couldn't return to life again. I had already been made one with Death.

HEINRICH: What does that mean?

STRANGER: What does that mean? I'll tell you. You see my spectacles. I wear them because people have told me that they cannot bear my gaze since I came out of prison, in other words, since I looked at Death. Since then I see all things with the eyes of Death, and you will understand that Death does not see anything in the same way as a living man.

HEINRICH: As far as I can see, you still are a living man.

STRANGER: As far as you can see, yes. But you still see very little. I know that you see far more than other men. For example, you see Death in the eyes of the young medical student.

HEINRICH: Quiet about that.

STRANGER: As you wish. – I was talking about my condemnation. I then learnt that Death is not an event, as you put it. Only those who have not really made its acquaintance, who have not been alone with it day and night, could say that. One night Death began to talk to me; I must tell you that he had a very quiet, indeed a very attractive, way of coming and speaking. He didn't terrify me at all – no hint of the skeleton or the tousled hair and fearful countenance about him. No, there was something reassuring about Death. I tell you, Death is a gentleman; he wants justice to be done, he takes care, he is reticent, and very reserved. We talked together for a long time. Then we became one.

HEINRICH: Madness!

STRANGER: It was only when I returned to freedom that I noticed what had happened to me. People and things didn't look the same as they had done before. I couldn't talk to anyone without seeing Death standing behind them. Each of their words seemed hollow, each laugh empty, their anger and their joy seemed meaningless. Without wanting to, without doing the least thing about it, I read in their eyes the time and circumstances of their end. I met my fiancée and immediately broke off our engagement. My mother took me in her arms; I pulled myself away, and that was the only time since that I have felt anything like tears in my eyes.

HEINRICH: Horrible.

STRANGER: Not as horrible as you think. Otherwise everything left me quite unexcited. Nothing could excite me, disquieten me; on the contrary, I felt as tranquil, as empty, as solemn and as indifferent as though I were in a strange cemetery. I really feel very well. No more passions, no surging of the heart, no hot blood – my heart beats as regularly as clockwork – no love, no friendship, no sympathy, no tears. I'm more than ever interested in people since I've seen how Death is looking over the shoulders of each one of them.

HEINRICH: So you want to say that you have second sight?

STRANGER: Yes and no. I've lost the first; I have only the second. So I don't suffer with it, like those who have second sight only occasionally and are terrified by it. You see, it simply is a question of clearing the table, making straightforward conditions. 'No man can serve two masters.'

HEINRICH: It's a very monotonous service that you're talking about.

STRANGER: On the contrary, young sir, on the contrary, it's very diverse and full of variety. It's not the result, what people call death, because they only see it then, that is interesting. What interests me is the slow but certain work of Death in men as long as they live, the dissolution, collapse, disintegration and corruption in the living body. It is dying that is interesting, not being dead, and dying lasts a long time and is as varied as life.

HEINRICH: I'm beginning to find this conversation repulsive.

STRANGER: I can believe that, young sir, and I will tell you why. You're one of the half-and-half people, the hasty ones, the weak. Granted, you know more than most – that's why I came to you – but you're making a serious mistake: you're splitting yourself in two. You see your death. Good, that's a beginning. But at the same time you're taking everything that you do and think deadly seriously; you're beginning to flounder, to writhe, to protest, to feel hurt, because Death is not as you depicted him. You reproach him for avoiding you when you looked for him and for looking for you since you've been avoiding him. You have marvellous games with the revolver, philosophize about what would be the 'noblest departure' for yourself. You very much like to have your fancy tickled a bit by Death. So things go on inside you, and you get nowhere. You want to serve two masters, you serve neither, and so you get your thrashing from both. It's a shame. You're dishonest. Your friend, this young medical student, is a different sort of chap.

HEINRICH: I tell you, keep quiet. If you yourself are unhappy and have to make people unhappy, at least leave me and others whom I do not know out of the game.

STRANGER: I'm really sorry to have to contradict you again. I'm not unhappy myself – I've already told you that –

nor do I make people unhappy. On the contrary, on the contrary! What do people want? Granted, there were times when they wanted to live, wanted to live under any circumstances, and then they made Death the skeleton with the scythe, they blasphemed and mocked him because they wanted to live for ever; then they made ordinances and laws which had the sole aim of preserving life; anyone who transgressed these ordinances and laws was condemned to death, so that the others might live. I openly concede that I can hardly put myself back into this period; I don't understand it. That's because I've lost my first sight. But today? Who still wants to live? A couple of lovers who fear that the world might collapse before they can consummate their love; a couple of fools who are drunk with their power and put up monuments to last for centuries. But all the rest? Which of them still blasphemes or mocks death? Do they not rather blaspheme and mock life? I once opened the Bible in prison; there I read the words 'They struggle for death' (Wisdom I. 12). That's a good saying. Men are like that today. They are not frightened of Death, they don't run away from it, but they seek it, they love it, they struggle for it . . . You can only make men happy today if you help them to find Death.

HEINRICH: Have you ever heard that people today are healthier and live longer than ever before?

STRANGER: Quite right; but you must understand that properly. The tactics of Death have changed with time. Earlier, when people lived in fear of him, he came suddenly, roughly, fearfully. He snatched infants from their mothers and young mothers from their children, annihilated whole villages in a few days with plague and all sorts of other devastations. Today, when Death is desired, he comes slowly, furtively, in gradual, barely perceptible, dissolution. In former times people took their lives by dagger or rope; today they take sleeping pills. In former days, men fought with their death all day long; today they go to sleep with morphia. Don't you see? Death adapts itself. In barbaric times, in which life is all that matters, Death is also barbaric. In civilized times, in which people have become honourable and wise, Death also meets them in a civilized way – of course, all this always with a pinch of salt. I'm saying all this simply to prove to you that I make men happy, not unhappy.

HEINRICH: You're offering me a strange mixture of understanding and madness. Don't you see how ordinary people today seek with all their strength to obtain their rights to life, to joy, to respect, to freedom? Is that not a will to live, which throws overboard all your theories?

STRANGER: You're coming to the main point, and you will probably be surprised if I tell you that I myself actively support these different efforts, indeed, that this is my main concern. I work as a functionary in numerous of these organizations, partly from idealism, partly as a business.

HEINRICH: You must get wages somewhere, and I've been wondering how you really manage to live.

STRANGER: Oh, don't worry about that, young sir. I can tell

you in confidence that death isn't a bad business. I give each person suitable advice; life assurance, or things that no one wants to pay; I warn them, and I speak to them. I'm not unknown to marriage bureaux, and I've already helped a number of people to an attractive, easily won legacy; also a bit of occultism; all in all, just enough for me to have what I need. But that is only – shall we say the material –

HEINRICH: Shall we say the dirty side of the business.

STRANGER: You're very strait-laced, young sir. Each man earns his wages according to his capabilities. But let's get back to the main point, to the concern of the mass for freedom, equal rights, food, and so on. I welcome it absolutely, and I encourage it; I'm interested in it as in all processes of dissolution and collapse. People have at last become sensible; they only want what confronts them in any case, Death. They even break the ordinances and laws which compulsorily kept them alive. Any servant who wants to be free of his master, any wife who wants to be free of her husband, any child who wants to be free of its parents, and trumpets it on the streets, works wholly for my cause – if you will allow me the expression. Any slut or fool who wants to have equal rights with the brave and wise does the same thing. Any man who has arranged his life in such a way as to enjoy it to the full contributes his share to the acceleration of the dissolution. Those barbaric times, in which men wanted above all else to live, could preserve life only with the strictest laws and the severest discipline. One can really hardly think of it without laughing. People wanted to live, and what did life consist of? Work, obedience, subordination, renunciation, privation, toil and tribulation, so that they themselves called it a vale of tears. Each one always lived only for the others, parents for children, children so that one day they would be parents, the lords for the slaves, and the slaves for the lords, one generation for the next, and the next for the one after that, no one – and this really is folly – quite simply and honestly for himself. Nevertheless, they loved life and called the whole thing – God's command, and they were happy in their own way. Today, in these civilized times, people have got beyond this sort of happiness. Today people are no longer bothered about living. Did they ask to be born? Who obliges them to live? Today we know that the greater happiness, indeed the only real enjoyment, lies in the dissolution of life. Marriage, family, authority, order, law, these things are only relics from barbaric times which stubbornly survive. Today men enjoy dying. I love the sweet smell of corruption. This is an unprecedented time for our sort, I can tell you. One must simply recognize the fact, and learn to exploit it. Do you understand, young sir? Co-operate. You will have your joy and your success in it. (*Knock at the door.*) I'm going. I only hope that your next visitor won't turn your head again. My regards. Good evening. (*As he goes out, Christoph comes in.*)

CHRISTOPH: What was he talking about?

HEINRICH: Our theme. Come in, sit down and have a drink.

CHRISTOPH: You're not surprised that I've come?

HEINRICH: No, I knew you would. One of us had to take the first step, and as you are the aristocrat, you came first.

CHRISTOPH: What does that mean?

HEINRICH: It's very simple. It didn't occur to you that you could forgive yourself something by coming first. Our kind first ask themselves a hundred times what sort of an impression it will make, how it will look, whether it will not be misunderstood. You don't need to, you're much too sure of yourselves for that. You simply come and suppose that the other person will somehow just be content with that, and if he still doesn't understand, then that doesn't bother you at all. So you are aristocrats. The rest of us are less trusting – and we have our experience. And after all, we still don't know one another.

CHRISTOPH: That's why I came. We must get to know one another.

HEINRICH: You're enviably blind. And you don't bother what someone else might think of you. Perhaps the other person doesn't want to get to know you, but that's all the same to you; you don't think that possible. You don't notice that your certainty is fundamentally a boundless contempt of people, and here you go modestly and quietly so as to disarm us completely. But you're still right about it; for we, too, quietly allow ourselves to be despised by you and even fancy ourselves for it.

CHRISTOPH: What you say isn't you. It's a strange voice.

HEINRICH: Yes, it's strange to you, but not to me. It's the voice of the common people, whom you so despise. It's a good thing that you've managed to hear it for once.

CHRISTOPH: Like you, I've rotted in a trench for four years; do you really think this voice is new to me? I know it well enough. But because it stems from mistrust, there is an impure, false tone to it; that's why it's bad. I haven't come to you to hear this voice, which isn't yours, but to talk with you as man to man.

HEINRICH: Man to man – you always say that when you want to silence the voice of the mass, the common people, which lives in us; this voice is irksome to you. You want to detach us from the community in which alone we have any being, and you know well enough that you need no longer fear us once you confront us as individuals. We are the mass, or nothing. Man to man? Let us first become men, then we will also talk to you as man to man.

CHRISTOPH (*after a while, pensively*): If a man despises himself, he also feels despised by others. Heinrich, let me speak to you frankly. As far as I know, our lives have been very different. I don't want to say that that is something unimportant. I hardly know the world in which you have grown up; our sort never get to know it thoroughly. But you don't know my world either. I come from a so-called good family, i.e. from an old, respected, bourgeois family, and I am not one of those who are ashamed to say so. On the contrary, I know the tranquil strength that there is in a good bourgeois home. No one can know that if they have not grown up in it. It's difficult to explain. But you must know one thing. We have become great by respecting what has happened and what is given, in other words, by respecting every man. We hold mistrust to be common and low. We look for the frank word and deed of the other man and we want to accept it without suspicion. The psychologizing and analysing of people which has now become fashionable means the destruction of all trust, the public calumniation of all that is decent, the revolt of all that is common against what is free and true. Men are not in a position to look into the depths of each other's heart – they still cannot do it – but they should encounter each other and each accept the other as he is, simply, candidly, in confident trust. Do you understand?

HEINRICH: I'm trying to, but it's difficult. Where am I to get this trust? What am I to ground it on? Do you think that we would not love to be able to live in trust towards people? Do you think that we enjoy our constant mistrust? But that is our trouble, that we cannot bring ourselves to have trust. Our experiences are bitter.

CHRISTOPH: A man's experiences are usually like the man himself. The mistrustful man will never make the venture of trust. Trust is always a leap forward beyond all good and bad experiences. But it may well be that this leap is harder for you than it is for me. So I came to you and did not wait for you. Besides, you mustn't think that we are blind in our trust, that we throw ourselves straight into the arms of any man. We leave that to those who drivel about the equality and goodness of all men. We have learnt to distinguish – and we will let no one stand in our way – to distinguish between authentic and unauthentic, true and false, noble and common, decency and exploitation.

HEINRICH: And is what you call authentic, true, noble, decent, something quite beyond question, something self-evident to you?

CHRISTOPH: There must be some self-evident things in life, and one must have the courage to stand by them. One cannot begin life from the beginning again every day, questioning everything that one learnt and assumed the day before. Our self-evident values have been tested by many generations, they have been proved by experience hundreds and thousands of times.

HEINRICH: Yes, in the life of your grandfathers. But times change.

CHRISTOPH: But men do not, at any rate, not in their essential character. That is the great mistake which people keep on making today. They think that the world only began with them, they question everything and never come to the point of contributing the small stone which is their share in the building of the whole.

HEINRICH: What's the use of stones if the foundations are collapsing?

CHRISTOPH: You talk like a journalist, and you should know better. If the foundations were really collapsing, then it would be a waste of time trying to lay them again. No people can lay its foundations for a second time after a thousand years of history. If the foundations collapse, all is up. But that is not the case. The foundations are deep and firm and good. One must simply build on them and not on the quicksand of so-called new ideas.

HEINRICH: Do not think that we, like the literati who make their money out of it, are concerned with new ideas. What are we looking for? We really have neither the time nor the inclination to look for originality at any price. We want something far simpler: ground under our feet, so that we can live. That's what I called the foundations. Don't you see the difference? You have a foundation, you have ground under your feet, you have a place in the world. For you there are self-evident values, for which you stand and for which you would gladly lay down your lives, because you know that your roots lie so deep that they will continue to sustain you. You are only concerned with one thing, to keep your feet on the ground. Otherwise you would be like the giant Antaeus, who received his strength only from the contact of his feet with the ground, and who lost it when Hercules lifted him up from the ground in a fight. True, there are also fools in your midst, who leave the ground of their own accord, out of curiosity, or vanity, or because they foolishly think that they will win us over in that way. Chaff, which the wind blows away. It's a question of having ground under one's feet if one wants to live, and we do not have this ground. So we are blown hither and thither with the storm. We have nothing for which we are able and willing to lay down our lives, and we cling to our miserable life, not because we love it, but because it is the only one that we have. – And if you have the threat of death by a splinter from a grenade, grinning at you daily, and you don't know why you are living or why you are dying, then it's a miracle if you are *not* frenzied with greed for life and despair, filled with hatred of everything living and a lust for wild enjoyment. Give me ground under my feet, give me the Archimedean point on which I can stand – and everything would be different.

CHRISTOPH (*who has become very pensive*): Ground under your feet – I never guessed. I think you're right. I understand – ground under your feet, to be able to live and to be able to die.

HEINRICH: Yesterday evening you said some very proud things about the mob, and I admitted their truth. There is a mob, and this mob must be kept under. But what is the offence of those who have been thrust into life without any ground under their feet? Can you pass by them and speak over their heads without being smitten with grief?

G.S.III pp. 478–95

Meanwhile correspondence passed between the Archbishop of Sweden and the Archbishop of Canterbury about a conference which had probably been proposed while Bonhoeffer was in Sweden on his abortive mission. The conference was to bring together churchmen from both sides of the struggle, after the war was over, to reconcile and rebuild. He was remembered by those who were planning this small conference in Sweden. The Swedish archbishop wrote from Uppsala to William Temple in Britain suggesting that such a conference might be called 'as soon as it seems possible to make arrangements'. This conference was to heal the wounds of war. A part of the letter is worth quoting:

13th February, 1943

ARCHBISHOP ERLING EIDEM TO ARCHBISHOP TEMPLE: I

may assure you that I reckon it as a privilege for the Church of Sweden and myself to summon a small representative conference as early as possible after the close of hostilities. I think it would be most useful that I, as a member of a neutral people, may send that invitation. I fully agree with you, my dear Archbishop and venerated friend, that it should be most useful that the invitations are individual, but naturally after friendly consultation of the bodies that should be represented. I think you are also quite right in your suggestion that those invited should have known each other before in the ecumenical movement.

It is not surprising that Bonhoeffer's name should appear in the first tentative list which Eidem received from George Bell, Bishop of Chichester. That list is contained in a letter of 3rd November, 1943:

CHICHESTER TO ARCHBISHOP EIDEM: I jot down my own collection of the names that you and I talked over at Uppsala last year; yourself, Berggrav, Fuglsang-Damgaard, Canterbury, Aubrey (perhaps vice Paton), Otto Dibelius, Wurm, Bonhoeffer, Niemöller, Boegner, Kramer, Koechlin, 't Hooft. The Americans I expect are best reached by contact with Cavert . . .

There is no indication that these men, who knew Bonhoeffer so well, had any idea that he was in prison. News travels slowly in wartime. Even his brother-in-law, Professor Leibholz, in Oxford, married to Dietrich's twin-sister, appears to know nothing of what is happening. From Robert Mackie he hears that Dietrich is well and in a letter of 21st April sends his 'warmest love' to him and tells of the confirmation of his eldest daughter, Dietrich's niece. Writing to Harry Johansson in Sweden, late in June, he is still sending greetings, with no knowledge of the arrest.

The plans for the post-war conference in Sweden thus proceeded without Bonhoeffer's knowledge and without any of the participants being aware that he had been arrested and was awaiting trial. He would most certainly have approved of the plans. This was why he returned to Germany in 1939 and as yet he had no idea that he would not be alive at the end of the war to co-operate in just such work. But, as we have seen, the idea of death occupied his attention. It was one of his steps on the road to freedom, even if he was not yet eager to take it! In fact he did not write the poem, 'Stations on the Road to Freedom', until a year later when the July Plot failed.

It is interesting to note how little attention Roeder, who was conducting the case against Bonhoeffer, gave to his contacts abroad. What seems to have concerned him most was the evasion of military service. He saw that Bonhoeffer had helped young pastors and officials of the Confessing Church out of military service by taking them into the Abwehr. *Names mentioned were Wilhelm Niesel, Ernst Wolf and the son of Wilhelm Jannasch. Roeder had found a letter of Bonhoeffer's to Dohnanyi, in which he anxiously asked help for Wilhelm Niesel, who was 'threatened' with the call-up. Bonhoeffer wrote to Roeder explaining this in June 1943:*

BONHOEFFER TO ROEDER: . . . I must admit that [the word 'threaten'] taken by itself does make a very disagreeable impression. On the other hand, I should like to say the following: 1. If a man like Niesel had come under an officially recognized church authority, it would undoubtedly have declared him indispensable for purely church reasons. 2. Only a Church whose faith has an inner strength can perform its grave service on behalf of its country during a war. But whatever one thinks of the Confessing Church, one thing can never be said of it without completely misunderstanding it, namely that in it the 'call-up' was ever regarded as a 'threat'. The hundreds of young pastors of the Confessing Church who volunteered and the large proportion of them who laid down their lives are a sufficiently eloquent testimony to the contrary.

Nor have I ever spoken to a single pastor of the Confessing Church who did not joyfully embrace his call-up as an inner liberation from the burden of political suspicion that rested on the Confessing Church. Most have eagerly sought the opportunity of proving their own attitude and readiness for self-sacrifice as a soldier. The fact that Pastor Niemöller volunteered for military service right at the beginning of the war had its effect on the Confessing Church . . . Because on this point we can have a very clear conscience, I thought that in an urgent particular case such as Niesel's I might, and, indeed, had to, act to preserve a pastor for the service of his Church and his country, provided that this could be justified on military grounds. It was not my job to know about the latter, which is why I consulted my brother-in-law. Many of my former pupils who have now been killed or are still at the front as soldiers have said that, despite their happiness at serving their country, they have one anxiety, namely that during this period the churches at home should be completely cared for . . . Two things influenced my action: I know that even religious men can have very different opinions concerning the Church, but, particularly in wartime, no one can deny that the motivating force behind its conviction and its action is love of the German people and the desire to serve it during the war in the best possible way. Since the beginning of the war I have had several long discussions with Minister Gürtner, whom I knew personally, and have asked that the Church Struggle be settled and that the various sections of the Evangelical Church should work together. I made suggestions to Dr Gürtner on this subject, which he then discussed with Kerrl, the Minister for Religious Affairs, who welcomed them with interest. In December 1940 Dr Gürtner explicitly told me, during a walk together in Ettal which lasted several hours, that he hoped to achieve this and the way in which he proposed doing so. His death a month later, and the illness and death of Minister Kerrl have destroyed this hope. It was an attempt to establish peace within the Church during the war in order to make the maximum energy available for its conduct. Even this unsuccessful attempt means that I may consider that I did whatever I could to achieve the smoothest and greatest possible war effort on the part of the Church. (*Quoted by Eberhard Bethge in the German edition of his biography, p. 920.*)

This first part of the imprisonment was dominated by the interrogation and Roeder's less than serious attention to the case. For him Bonhoeffer was 'small fry'.

B] AUGUST 1943–APRIL 1944

The second period was after the charge had been made. The change of atmosphere is seen in Bonhoeffer's sense of relief, his request for a lawyer, and his conviction that it would not be long before he was released. The most descriptive letter of that period came right at the beginning, to his parents, 3rd August, 1943. It says much about his state of mind. He expresses his pleasure at being able to write more often. He discusses the trivia of prison inconveniences, makes light of his troubles and assures his parents that they need not worry. He is reading, apparently untroubled by fears of a conviction. He is only impatient at his inactivity and wants to be out and doing.

On 25th September, 1943, a regular warrant was made for his arrest. He was now officially charged with anti-war activity. The trial was expected on 17th December, 1943. Dohnanyi's illness delayed it and Bonhoeffer was very disappointed that he was not tried despite this. He wanted to get the matter over and done with. He had little fear of being found guilty. Bethge quotes an important letter of this period which illustrates his disappointment and impatience:

BONHOEFFER TO BETHGE: About myself, I am sorry to have to tell you that I am not likely to be out of here before Easter. No change can be made while Hans is sick. I cannot help feeling that there has been a lot of messing about and dreaming while the simplest things have been left undone. I'm sure that everyone concerned has meant well . . . I am simply amazed that for the last six months nothing has actually been done, although people have obviously sacrificed a great deal of time and sleep on my account with their deliberations and their discussions. The only thing that could have taken place automatically, namely that my case be settled before Christmas, has been prevented . . .   (*From Bethge's biography*)

It was about this time that he tried his hand at writing a novel. His earlier attempt at a drama had not been completed and one gets the impression that Bonhoeffer was seeking to find a form in which he could cast his thoughts. From the draft for the novel, two conversations have been published:

TWO CONVERSATIONS FROM THE ATTEMPT AT A NOVEL (1943-4)

I

'. . . I want to say something to you, Franz; perhaps you can still take advantage of it. In what we were talking about it's not just a matter of style, but of much more. It's no good being prudish; you can't learn a tough job like being a soldier without coarse language, without an occasional curse, indeed without a robust wit. It's often very difficult for anyone who hasn't been used to it all along. But he must grit his teeth and learn that there are other kinds of people and other ways of living. Perhaps he will even succeed in prevailing against the majority – if so, all the better; but that's not necessary, and no one should be too distressed about it; that doesn't help. A man must know that there is a great deal of coarseness and obscenity in life, and he must cope with it and still remain the person he is . . .' [Franz:] 'For two years I've been helping a former pastor who resigned from the ministry so as to be able to spend all his time working in the poor quarters of our town. I took over a youth club there and had to visit the homes of the parents of my young people. In doing that I heard and saw more than I can say, and I know that people go through coarseness and guilt quite innocently, and I've found goodness and much readiness to help amongst them, without their losing a word of it.'

'Good', said the Major tersely. 'Incidentally, I doubt whether there's much point in doing that sort of work; but don't let's bother about that now. Anyone who gets excited over every coarse word is an old maid, and we don't want anything to do with them. But it's something quite different when a man exploits the power he has been given over other men to humble them, humiliate them, defile them and break them. That's no longer a matter of style; that's a sin both against men and against the office which one holds. It's the flouting of all true authority, and the destruction of all human fellowship; it's the fatal road to anarchy. Franz, I don't know where it comes from, but inside all of us there is a dark, unhealthy urge to misuse the authority which has been given to us and thus to destroy life, ours and others'. We must direct all our hate, all our passion against this really evil urge, wherever we meet it; first in ourselves, for do not think, Franz, that it is not also in you. It is just lurking for an opportunity to have its fling. It is quite uncanny that there must be power, indeed that power is something holy, from God, and yet it so easily makes us devils. Look at these petty forestry assistants; each a friendly, harmless, benevolent companion among his own folk, perhaps even a good, faithful, devoted father of a family. But each is a Satan when he feels the itch of his ludicrous bit of power, and a wretched creeper to his superiors. There are many burdens, but none that brings greater misfortune on men than the misuse of power, especially by petty people. Again and again history has produced great tyrants; they conjured up great counter-forces and rarely escaped their judgement; they are demigods, who are subject to no usual, human judgement. They rise and fall in a few years, but the petty tyrants do not die. They live in the favour of their particular master and sun themselves in it, and by so doing they escape all earthly judgement. The petty tyrants are the ones who wreck the very heart of a people; they are like invisible compulsions to destruction, bringing secret ruin to a young, flourishing life. Not only are they more dangerous; they are also stronger, rougher, harder to catch than the great. If one wants to grab them, they slip through one's fingers, for they are smooth and cowardly. They are really like an infectious disease. When a petty tyrant has sucked the life-blood from his victim, he has at the same time infected him with his spirit; and as soon as the one who was hitherto merely a victim of oppression gets the least power into his hands he takes vengeance for what has happened to him. But this vengeance – and that is the frightful thing – is taken, not on the guilty, but once again only on the innocent, helpless victims, and so it goes on *ad infinitum*, until everything is infected and poisoned and collapse cannot be held off any longer.' The Major stopped and took a breath. 'Nevertheless', he continued, 'one should not be disheartened by the apparent pointlessness of the struggle. Anyone who has succeeded in bringing about the downfall of one of these petty, evil spirits may congratulate himself on having saved many human lives. He has become a benefactor to mankind, even if no one is aware of it. Many well-disposed members of our class have grown used to laughing at these petty tyrants and think that anyone who has declared all-out war on them is a fool. But it is as foolish and irresponsible to laugh at them as it is to laugh at bacteria, because *they* are small, and at the doctor who saves the life of one or two sick people and in so doing himself falls victim to the plague. True, there must also be strategists and soldiers in this war, as there have to be in war against the plague, people who investigate the cause of the illness with the microscope, and others who, as doctors, attack individual cases. But woe to anyone who mocks at the sacrifices which are made in this war! . . .'

II

[The Major has just been talking about the rivalry between the father of the young men he is talking to, and himself, at school.] 'Each one thought that the other was in his way and had to be suppressed. If one wanted to be pretentious, one might say that it was a pure struggle for power. Of course, neither of us knew that, but with things as they were, the clash was inevitable. When we awoke from our dream, we had learnt that no man is in the world alone, by himself, but that he has to live alongside other men and get on with them, and that this is a good thing for people. Of course, one has to give up some things, to learn to compromise without surrendering one's character; indeed one's character is only formed in this sort of encounter.'

The attention with which the young men were listening to these words of the Major was a tacit demand that he should go into rather more detail on this point.

'You will', said the Major, turning to the young men, 'continually meet people in your life – perhaps you yourselves are still among them – who think it full of character to suppress any rebellion, any opposition, any expression of non-conformity immediately, with force. Indeed such are proud of finding rebellion and enmity because they give them an occasion of showing their power. It is therefore a question of "much enmity, much honour", and "compromise is characterless", etc. That all sounds very splendid, but it's third-form stuff. Only people who don't have any eye for human relationships, any contact with reality, any feeling for existing values, talk like that. Eternal third-formers. They judge their own power only by the ruins that they leave behind them; they think it meritorious to shatter as much fine porcelain as possible, and they rejoice in childish glee over the breaking of window-panes. They regard it as the sign of a strong character never to retreat a step, never to get out of anyone's way, never to make a compromise. As long as we are children we may surrender ourselves to such dreams of our petty selves dominating the world, delight in our naïvety that we even find a following because others believe our dream. But what sort of a following is that! Weaklings, hypocrites, and at best dreamers! But the sooner we learn that this is sin against life itself, the better. Anyone who has not learnt that by the time he has grown up is a disaster to his fellow-men and to himself.

'To knock another man's head in simply because he is different, whether in imagination or in reality, has very little to do with character. In fact it needs a great deal more character to understand and get on with someone else without betraying oneself in the process. Getting on together without knocking each other's head in is the real task of life. How naïve those people are who see only weakness and cowardly surrender in that! No, this is where the real battle is fought and won, and it is often rough, long, infinitely wearisome, before one gets a step further forward. What is it about, then? Not about leaving the other person like a corpse on the battlefield, but about struggling to gain his agreement with one's own will, or, better, about achieving a common will between the two of you, about making a friend out of an enemy. This will never succeed without restraint on both sides, above all, it will never succeed without mutual recognition and respect. Here alone is the field on which character shows itself and develops. Nothing is destroyed here; it is rather built up. It is no dream or fantasy world, but the world of men's real communal life together. Here, too, power and strength are exerted, not for their own sakes, but in the service of a self-understanding, a better common life among men. Excuse me, I'm getting worked up, but I believe that a young man cannot learn all this too soon. We Germans so easily miss life, not from wickedness, but from dreaming, delight in words, ideas and feelings. We find it more difficult to get together than others do. We remain individuals who fight among each other to the point of drawing blood over the slightest differences – or we surrender ourselves completely, subject ourselves utterly to the will of a single individual. But both these ways are sins against life itself, and they must fail. Life requires us to be together, and we find that hard. That is what Hans and I learnt at the age of fourteen, and we have never forgotten it.'

Now Franz joined in the conversation. What Uncle had said reminded him of his old history teacher from the first form; he was the only teacher whom he had loved and honoured; he was very wise, and unlike the other teachers (from whom he had heard only platitudes). He was a really educated, sensitive, tranquil man. All that he was he showed in a great good will, indeed a goodness that one could understand, towards each of his pupils. He had tried to do justice to each of those who had a serious opinion about anything. It was only when they spread gossip or uttered platitudes that he could become dreadfully angry. 'Still, I could never agree with him', said Franz, and he very much wanted to know whether Uncle had meant basically the same things as this teacher. Some things had reminded him very much of his teacher, others had not. 'I shall never forget the way in which he showed us the great movements in history, the French Revolution, the Reformation, the rise of Christianity. These lessons still reconcile me to schooldays which in other respects were quite wasted. But when the teacher had got to the end of this material, there were some lessons in which the consequences were to be drawn. The teacher had seemed to become another man in these lessons; whereas earlier he had spoken with fire and passion, he was now overcome with a certain heaviness. He said that history showed that all these great movements and ideas had ultimately brought misfortune to men. The French Revolution had ended in terror and was the beginning of mob-rule in Europe; the Reformation had ultimately destroyed the spiritual unity of the West and in the end had left it unprotected against materialism; Christianity had shattered the inner life of nations and individuals, and so hardly anyone had found himself any more. But to prevent the catastrophe, in the end each time there had been a moderate compromise between the world and the new ideas, and precisely the characteristic elements which had originally provided the driving force had been buried. One could never say this without being branded by society as a heretic and an enemy of the people. But probably everything was basically right and good as it was, and in any case it was the result of the lesson of history and of life and we should learn that people can only live by compromise. I once retorted that one could equally justifiably describe what he had called the results of history as the phenomena of its dissolution and decline. Why, in that case, should one snuffle around in the putrefying stink of history instead of keeping to its great periods and recognizing in them the results and lessons of history?'

'You're certainly a very skilful dialectician', interjected the Major, with a laugh, 'but it's still only playing with words.'

'That's almost exactly what my teacher also said', continued Franz. 'Words were not important – one had to remain true to reality, and honest, and have no illusions. To do this, one also had to have a clear picture of the so-called great periods. They looked very fine afterwards, but that was simply the great deceit of the historians, who were too cowardly to look the facts in the face. For ninety-nine per cent of those who had to live through such great periods they were a chain of sorrow and misery, and one might call it good fortune that a generation was only blighted by such a "great period" every other century. "What sort of right, then," he shouted passionately, "have we to look at history always from the standpoint of a few successful people and to forget the blood and tears of the millions? I tell you, Franz, this history-writing is barbarous, something for oriental despots of two thousand years ago, but a moral scandal after two thousand years of Christianity. It is this history-writing which continually produces new barbarism, because it systematically coarsens men and makes them common." I had nothing to say in reply and was very impressed. "It is the moral of the so-called great periods", my teacher continued, "that man, his life and his fortune are worth nothing, indeed, that human blood must be poured out to consecrate the altar of the idol of some idea. Do not misunderstand me," he cried almost solemnly, "I am saying nothing against the great ideas and the great men in history; both are semi-divine beings and forms which from time to time intervene in the history of earthly men according to a plan which we cannot understand; they are both glorious and fearful at the same time, glittering and destructive. Anyone who wants to understand the great ideas of history as the result of hunger, and the great men as products of the masses, is childish. He can understand nothing of their superhuman power and fearfulness. It is presumption and folly to criticize them. No, I bow down before these incomprehensible powers which – according to the wisdom of Holy Scripture – derive from the forbidden intercourse of sons of God with daughters of men (Gen. 6. 4). The race of giants of whom the sagas of our peoples tell are still alive, and from time to time can be seen on our earth. We are dwarfs before them. Yes, dwarfs. Mark it well. But for that very reason we should not act as though we were giants. For that reason let no one talk to me about the 'great periods'. They are the arenas of mythical, semi-divine figures, but for the rest of us they are fearful, indeed in truth even the giants perish in them. Jesus, Luther, Cromwell, Robespierre, Napoleon – none of them really sought human happiness, even if they talked about it, and each of them, like Jesus, cried at the end of his own life-work, 'My God, my God, why hast thou forsaken me?' " '

The Major had listened attentively to Franz, whose ardour had increased as he spoke. Now he interrupted him with the remark which had been made just before. 'A wise man, your teacher, but the last remark was false. He should have excluded Christ; and in that case everything else looks different.' Franz threw an astonished and somewhat uncomprehending look at the Major but once again continued his narrative, which was really only meant to be a question. 'As I knew of no other help, I asked our teacher whether in that case men were made to be happy. He looked at me with a friendly, yet sorrowful gaze, behind which there was almost a slight smile, and spoke almost like a child. He didn't really know that, nor did he know whether there was anyone who knew, but he would like to talk about it with me again, in about twenty years, and then perhaps we would both know more. He died soon after. Perhaps now he does know more . . . And so I wanted to ask

you, Uncle Harald, whether with your remarks about getting
on together you meant that people can only live by compromise. I would find that frightful', he added, almost boyishly.

'You've raised more questions than we could discuss round
a coffee-table, Franz', said the uncle. 'I agree with your teacher
in many things, particularly in what he said about the great
periods of history and about history-writing. It is true enough,
the history of success has been written more or less completely,
and there is probably nothing very important to add. But is it
now time – and this is a far more difficult task – to write the
history of failures and the history of the victims of success, in
other words, to use your teacher's language, not the history of
giants and demigods, but of men? I don't mean the history of
the eternally unresting and rebellious masses, the clashes and
explosions; they too are superhuman, though also subterra-
nean, mythical forces, which have some mysterious connection
with the great successes of history. No, I mean the history of
men who have attempted to lead their lives, with work, family,
sorrow and happiness, thrown between these two forces. I've
told you about Hans and myself. We both thought we were
demigods until we knew, or at any rate suspected, that we
were men, who had to live and take notice of each other, with
each other and alongside each other; and that was our good
fortune. We became friends. Demigods have no friends, they
only have instruments which they use or throw away according
to their whim. I mistrust any man who has no friend. Either
he is a demigod or, far worse, he imagines that he is one. For
me, the chief thing about men and nations is whether they
have learnt to live with other men and nations or not. That is
more important to me than all their ideas, thoughts and convictions, and your history teacher probably meant very much
the same thing. I would not, however, say that the result of
history and of life was compromise. Anyone who talks like

that is still looking only at ideas. So he must continually discover that no idea is put into practice in its pure form. As a result, he calls that compromise and sees it simply as a sign of the imperfection and wickedness of the world. I confine my attention to man and his task of living with other men, and I see the fulfilment of human life and history as consisting precisely in the fulfilment of this task. What seems misfortune to your teacher is in my eyes people's only happiness. They do not have to live with ideas and principles and statements of faith and morals; they can live together, meeting each other and showing one another their proper tasks simply in this process of encounter. Only this kind of life is a fruitful one and a human one.

'You can't imagine the change that took place after the contest, not only in Hans and me, but also in the whole class. I was at Hans' bedside every day for a week; we got to know each other there and to see the world in a completely new way. Then a new life began in class. The spell which had been on the class as a result of Hans' character, which had been strengthened still further by my arrival, was broken. The capabilities and personalities of our contemporaries could develop. Whereas previously there had been only subservience, now there developed a healthy, firm friendship. Even Meyer, who was to be expelled from the school and only obtained a reprieve through Hansen's intervention, tried to join in, but he had to begin all over again from the bottom. He was later removed from school on other, unpleasant grounds. Hans remained form prefect until we left, but only as *primus inter pares*, and he made no decision without consulting the class thoroughly about it. Was that a compromise that was made between Franz and me? I wouldn't give it that name, because that would be to devalue it. The decisive thing was not what we both lost, namely our claim to be alone in the world as demigods, but what we gained, namely a human life in fellowship with other people. I now believe that the same thing also applies to nations, indeed basically to all historical movements. Let me put it in a rather different way from your school-teacher. Like nature, history develops superfluous forces for achieving a modest, but necessary, end. Look at the thousands of chestnuts which the candles on the trees promise us; how many of them will fulfil their purpose of growing into new chestnut trees? Hardly one. Nature is wasteful in order to be certain. It is just the same with the powerful movements of history, conflicts, revolutions, reformations, wars, whose end seems to be quite unrelated to the forces which are exerted. History too is wasteful when it is concerned with preserving the human race; it summons up the most tremendous forces to compel people to a single necessary insight. Even if we see and lament the incomprehensible failure in the relationship between the apparently senseless, unfruitful sacrifices and the modest result, we should never underrate the importance of even the most modest result. It is like the one chestnut out of thousands which invisibly takes root in the ground and again promises to bear fruit. Granted, the comparison is a lame one; history is not the same thing as nature. But the principle "all or nothing" doesn't hold for either. Instead, there is the law of preservation, the development and the fulfilment of life, even at the price of great sacrifice and renunciation. If there is any consequence, any lesson in history, I would not call it compromise, but the love of real life.' The Major took a deep breath and leant back . . .

'At each word that you spoke, Uncle Harald,' Christoph began, 'it seemed as though the ground was being taken from under my feet, as though I was walking on the sea. You call the love of real life, living together and getting on together, the ultimate basis of history and life. But what if forces are already at work which make it impossible to live together and get on together in any way, indeed, are intended to make this very thing impossible? What if a war has already been declared in which there can be no agreement, but only victory or submission? What if a power is rising up against us – like a monster which hitherto has been asleep – which seeks the annihilation of everything that has made life valuable and important to us? What if we have to recognize in this power no less than the destruction of all the ordinances of life, if we have to see in it the incarnation of evil itself? In that case, yes, in that case it can no longer be a matter of getting on with one another at any price – in that case it's a question of the content of life, of man's ultimate convictions, values and standards, and consequently of that "all or nothing" which you so condemn; in that case, anyone who avoids the issues will be a traitor to himself, his past, his calling and his own people. I believe that there is far too much false peace among men from which we must startle them. People look for men who dare to put a firm standard in their hands, who have the courage to live in accordance with it and to fight for it. And we, we ought to be the ones who put ourselves at the head and take the lead in the fight, for we know what we are defending and what our aim is. And because most people are slow and cowardly, there must be masters and servants, indeed I almost said slaves.' 'Christoph!' shouted Franz in extreme agitation, 'What you say is quite dreadful. You're getting worse even by your own standards.' 'Please let me have my say. I know you think otherwise', replied Christoph vigorously.

'Yes, I think that Aristotle's doctrine that some people are born to be slaves is right and that Schiller's revolutionary saying about man who is free "even if he were born in chains" is wrong. But for the small group of masters, for the free, the élite, the leaders, love for life and happiness may not be the ultimate standard. An unhappy man is better than a happy pet. I've just been reading the story of Don Quixote and Sancho Panza . . .' 'I'll be damned', shouted the Major, now half laughing and half in earnest, putting his hands in front of his face, 'but go on, Christoph, do go on.' Christoph flushed, but he immediately pulled himself together and continued his remarks to the end. 'I wanted to say that we cannot put philosophical and moral weapons into the hands of the Sancho Panzas, of whom there are more than enough among us.' 'O dear, O dear', cried the Major again. 'Now I've met my match. Don Quixote has thrown me from my horse. I'm one of the Sancho Panzas, I'm an *Epicuri de grege porcus*, an arch-Philistine, banausic. O Christoph, Christoph, what have you done to me? Don't be cross, I beg you. You are right, right in many things. But', and the Major shook his head and became quite serious, 'what a marvellous generation you are. You wise young people throw the things that we were enthusiastic about at your age, freedom and brotherliness among men, on the refuse-heap as childish illusions. Events cast their shadow forwards; before a hard winter the forest grows a thicker coat and the beaver puts on a thicker layer of fat. What sort of times and what sort of tasks are in store for a generation which already has to think so hard in its youngest days in order to survive? It makes one shudder. But Christoph, dear Christoph, if you must be hard, do not glory in hardness. If you must be inexorable in order to have your own way, do not forget to excuse yourself and to give way whenever it is possible. If you must despise life to gain it, don't forget to love it when you have gained it. And above all, beware of speaking lightly of happiness and flirting with unhappiness. That is contrary to nature, contrary to life, to man as he has been made, living his life as a poor sinner and longing for happiness as a small sign of God's good will. It is not as easy as you think

to be unhappy, and anyone who really is unhappy doesn't
despise and slander the happy. Please, I beg of you, Christoph,
none of this wild and arrogant talk about unhappy men and
happy pets. Why do you want to be masters, to lead, to be
ready to endure unhappiness if not in order to make other
people happy? Unhappiness comes by itself, or rather from
God; we don't have to run after it. To be unhappy is fate, but
to want to be unhappy – that's blasphemy and a serious illness
of the soul. Men have had too much of happiness, so now, for
a change, out of curiosity, they're making eyes at unhappiness.
I can't think of anything more blasé and, if you like – though
I hate to see this word misused – bourgeois than to ogle at
unhappiness. It's a dangerous product of boredom and a
profound lack of thought. Christoph, you're right in many
things that you've said about our time and our tasks – but one
must also be strong and upright enough not to make a virtue
out of necessity. Otherwise one is turning the world upside
down, and it will not stand it.'

The Major sank back in his chair, and it looked as though a
bitter memory had completely taken hold of him. 'You've
been saying something very dangerous, Christoph', he said
gently. 'Perhaps it's necessary for Germany, but – it's playing
with fire. Anyone who understands you wrongly can bring
about unspeakable disaster.' What the Major was thinking
about in these words, only his family could know, and the
young visitors felt that he had touched on something whose
significance they could not yet understand.

While he was speaking, Christoph had not noticed the
change that had come over Renate . . . He had, as he immediately recognized, opened up a deep gulf between himself
and her with his words. Renate had expected help from him,
and he had only thrust her deeper into her uncertainty. He
had given of the best of himself in what he had said. This was

the way in which he saw Germany and the task of his generation. But Renate had perceived in it the voice of the young
Germany in which she suffered, indeed which terrified her,
and seemed to make it impossible for her ever to be at home
here. Had she understood it properly? Had his remarks about
the born masters and born slaves some inward connection
with the appearance of the young forester which Christoph
abhorred no less than Renate? Was Renate confusing this
gruesome caricature of all rule with rule itself? Was what
Christoph really thought so easy to misunderstand, indeed,
were such caricatures perhaps the inevitable consequences if
little people took on great ideas? Why had not only Renate,
but also the Major, become so noticeably serious? . . .

G.S.III pp. 496–512

*In those conversations one can hear the echo of Bonhoeffer's concern
for his own battle. He did not fear trial, but sought it. The letters
which came out of prison when published in England had the
colourless title of* Letters and Papers from Prison, *but in German
the title came from a letter of this period –* Resistance and Submission. *This refers not to the struggle, but to the vacillating, which
was harder for Bonhoeffer to bear than prison itself!*

c] APRIL–SEPTEMBER, 1944

*In the third phase Bonhoeffer gave up any hope of an early date
being set for the trial. He even lost interest in it:*

7th May, 1944

I even quite forget it for weeks on end!

*His interest now turned to the July Plot. Bonhoeffer could only
observe now and follow events with rising excitement. There are
naturally no overt references to the plot, but he used the code name*

235

'Klaus' for it in his letters and showed his enthusiasm for it. Then it failed. Before that failure Bonhoeffer had obviously been encouraged by the visit of his uncle, General von Hase. Whether they talked of the coming coup *of the East Prussian General Headquarters or not, Bonhoeffer detected a new confidence in the resistance. Like many others he was shattered by the failure and the apparent invincibility of Hitler. A deeply moving and personal letter from Tegel was written on 21st July. It was to Eberhard Bethge and contains his attempt to define 'worldliness'. It also reaffirms Bonhoeffer's confidence in his last published book,* The Cost of Discipleship. *He claims that although he has changed, he would still stand by what he wrote then. Bonhoeffer was feeling for a base and he found it, at least temporarily, in a reconsideration of* The Cost of Discipleship.

Karl Barth, writing to P. W. Herrenbruck, comments on the Letters and Papers from Prison *and recalls Bonhoeffer as he knew him:*

What an open and rich and at the same time deep and disturbed man stands before us – somehow shaming and comforting us at the same time. That is how I also personally remember him. An aristocratic Christian, one might say, who seemed to run on ahead in the most varied dimensions. That is why I always read his earlier writings, especially those which apparently or in reality said things which at once were not clear to me, with the thought that – when they were seen round some corner or another – he might be right! So too with these letters, parts of which of course astonish me too. One cannot read them without having the impression that there might be something in them.

World Come of Age p. 131

Barth called these letters, 'a particular thorn in the flesh'. He did not like them, but he was forced to consider them and to question whether perhaps there was 'something in them'. His instinct to read Bon-

hoeffer's earlier writings was shrewd. The 'letters' have led to most misunderstanding because they have frequently been read first. Then Bonhoeffer's earlier writings are made to fit in with them, or are discarded. In fact, before turning to these important, but puzzling, letters, it is well to read carefully what led up to them. And no document is more important here than that regrettably unfinished book on Ethics. It emerged from the period 1940–43. The edition that we have was pieced together by the only man who had the right to do so. Eberhard Bethge had heard much of this book and Bonhoeffer trusted him to fill in the gaps. However incomplete it may be as a book, it is invaluable as a guide to the mind of Bonhoeffer before his arrest. This does not change overnight. His first letter to Bethge from prison expresses annoyance that he was not able to finish his Ethics. When we have read that book and carefully studied it we are in much better state to understand the 'letters'. It is a continuation of his earlier thinking, and as we have them these 'letters' are mere fragments of what might have been a powerful edifice. The fragments, Letters and Papers from Prison, are easily available and I shall not quote them here.

2. The End

On 22nd September, 1944, files were discovered in the air-raid shelter of the Abwehr *at Zossen. Before the 20th July, 1944, Bonhoeffer's fate seemed bearable, and offered some hope for his future; but this vanished when the bomb thrown in Hitler's headquarters killed some of his entourage, but not the tyrant himself. The countless meetings and discussions which prepared the* coup *d'état of the 20th July could be successfully kept dark; but its failure automatically brought about the discovery and liquidation of all those who had started, and carried on for years, the struggle against Hitler. So on 8th October, 1944, Dietrich Bonhoeffer was taken from the military prison in Tegel to the prison in the Gestapo headquarters. A fellow-prisoner reports:*

There I saw him for the first time at night when during an air-raid we prisoners were taken from our cells to a cement shelter in the prison yard. This was not done from humane considerations, to protect our lives, but the Gestapo feared we might be killed by a bomb before they had forced the information out of us which they hoped to get.

I must admit I was filled with alarm when I caught sight of Dietrich Bonhoeffer. But when I saw his upright figure and his imperturbable glance, I took comfort, and I knew that he had recognized me without losing his composure. First he was in cell 19. The very next morning I was able to have a word with him in the washroom which had facilities for several people, though the rule was that the prisoners were not allowed to speak to one another, and this was normally strictly watched. We had known each other for some time before the war began, and our relationship had become even closer through Dietrich Bonhoeffer's engagement to my cousin, Maria von Wedemeyer. Dietrich let me know immediately that he was determined to resist all the efforts of the Gestapo, and to reveal nothing of what our friends' fates made it our duty to keep dark.

A few days later he was transferred from cell 19 to cell 24. This made him my neighbour, and gave us the chance to communicate with one another and have short conversations every day. In the mornings we hurried together into a niche of the washroom where we could have a shower, and we eagerly indulged in this opportunity, though the water was cold, for in this way we could escape the supervision of our warders and have a brief exchange of thoughts. In the evenings this was repeated, and the doors of our cells remained open until all the prisoners of our corridor had returned. During that time we were eagerly talking to one another through the slits in the hinges of the door separating us. Finally, we saw one another during the air-raid warnings which happened every day and night, and where we seized every opportunity to inform each other of our thoughts and experiences.

Only someone who has been in strict solitary confinement for a long period of time is able to understand what this chance of talking to somebody meant for us during those long months. Dietrich Bonhoeffer told me of his interrogations: how the very first time they had threatened to apply torture, and with what brutality the proceedings were carried through. He characterized his interrogations with one short word: disgusting. His noble and pure soul must have suffered deeply. But he betrayed no sign of it. He was always good-tempered, always of the same kindliness and politeness towards everybody, so that to my surprise, within a short time, he had won over his warders, who were not always kindly disposed.

It was significant for our relationship that he was rather the hopeful one while I now and then suffered from depressions.

He always cheered me up and comforted me, he never tired of repeating that the only fight which is lost is that which we give up. Many little notes he slipped into my hands on which he had written biblical words of comfort and hope. He looked with optimism at his own situation too. He repeatedly told me the Gestapo had no clue to his real activities. He had been able to trivialize his acquaintance with Goerdeler. His connection with Perels, the justiciary of the Confessing Church, was not of sufficient importance to serve as an indictment. And as for his foreign travels and meetings with English Church dignitaries, the Gestapo did not grasp their purpose and point. If the investigations were to carry on at the present pace, years might pass till they reached their conclusions.

He was full of hope, he even conjectured that he might be set free without a trial, if some influential person had the courage to intercede on his behalf with the Gestapo. He also thought he had represented his relation to his brother-in-law, *Reichsgerichtsrat* von Dohnanyi, in a plausible way to his interlocutors, so that this was not a heavy charge against him. When Dohnanyi was also delivered to the Prinz-Albrecht-Strasse prison, Dietrich even managed to get in touch with him. When we returned after an air-raid warning from our cement shelter, his brother-in-law lay on a stretcher in his cell, paralysed in both legs. With an alacrity that nobody would have believed him capable of, Dietrich Bonhoeffer suddenly dived into the open cell of his brother-in-law. It seemed a miracle that none of the warders saw it. But Dietrich also succeeded in the more difficult part of his venture, in emerging from Dohnanyi's cell unnoticed and getting into line with the column of prisoners who were filing along the corridor. That same evening he told me that he had agreed with Dohnanyi upon all essential points of their further testimony.

Only once he thought things had taken a turn for the

worse, for he had been threatened with the arrest of his fiancée, his aged parents and his sisters unless his statements were more comprehensive. Then he judged the time had come frankly to declare that he was an enemy of National Socialism. His attitude, so he had stated, was rooted in his Christian convictions. In his talks with me he stuck to his opinion that no evidence could be produced which justified a prosecution for high treason.

As neighbours in our prison cells we also shared joy and sorrow in our personal and human life. The few things which we possessed and which we were allowed to accept from our relations and friends we exchanged according to our needs. With shining eyes he told me of the letters from his fiancée and his parents whose love he felt near him even in the Gestapo prison. Each Wednesday he received his laundry parcel, which also contained cigars, apples or bread, and he never omitted to share them with me the same evening when we were not watched; it delighted him that even in prison you were able to help your neighbour, and let him share in what you had.

On the morning of 3rd February, 1945, an air-raid turned the city of Berlin into a heap of rubble; the buildings of the Gestapo headquarters were also burnt out. Tightly squeezed together, we were standing in our air-raid shelter when a bomb hit it with an enormous explosion. For a second it seemed as if the shelter were bursting and the ceiling crashing down on top of us. It rocked like a ship tossing in the storm, but it held. At that moment Dietrich Bonhoeffer showed his mettle. He remained quite calm, he did not move a muscle, but stood motionless and relaxed as if nothing had happened.

I Knew Dietrich Bonhoeffer pp. 226–30

It is clear that despite his optimism Bonhoeffer knew that far more information was now available to the Gestapo since the discovery of the papers at Zossen. Eberhard Bethge, himself very close to the

events, tells how he discovered how much was known:
In November 1944 the interrogations that I myself was undergoing in the branch of the Head Office situated in the Kurfürstenstrasse brought me dangerously close to Bonhoeffer's case. Strange though it may seem, Commissar Baumer had concerned himself throughout my examination almost exclusively with my connections with Rüdiger Schleicher, but one afternoon he laid a thick typewritten file in front of me and showed me Bonhoeffer's signature on the last page. He said the file contained Bonhoeffer's confessions, and read out to me several passages from it. Among them I recognized parts of the Freiburg discussions of 1942 which dealt with the possibilities of contact between German and English churches in the event of a long armistice being arranged. All this information was not unfamiliar to me. I later learned that Gunther and Baumer placed the same file before Perels and Walter Bauer during similar interrogations. I denied all knowledge of the contents of this file. I knew that Bonhoeffer had been able to hide the fact of our close association in the past, and I assumed that he would not, in any case, have made such a detailed confession. I also knew from my own experience of the interrogations that minutes were kept and signed in seven copies. I therefore came to the conclusion that the whole file had been put together by the Gestapo from pieces of evidence obtained in various ways and that one of Bonhoeffer's signatures had then been added to it. Baumer soon returned to the subject of my frequent presence in the Schleicher household, which could be explained away convincingly enough by my engagement and marriage to Rüdiger Schleicher's daughter. He never again brought up the question of my relations with Dietrich Bonhoeffer.

Dietrich Bonhoeffer p. 805

Bethge is convinced that Bonhoeffer continued his theological work almost to the end, but there are no documents left.

On 4th January, 1945, Kaltenbrunner wrote a letter to the Head Office, which is the only document to survive about Bonhoeffer's interrogation:

The Protestant minister Dietrich Bonhoeffer, formerly chaplain to the German Evangelical Congregation in London, who was arrested in connection with the conspiracy of 20.7.1944, went to Sweden and had meetings with Lord Bishop Bell of Chichester during May and June 1942 by order of the former Admiral Canaris. Bonhoeffer has given the following information concerning the nature of his discussions with Bell:

Lord Bishop Bell, the most respected and best-known of the Lord Bishops of the Church of England, and influential in the ecumenical movement, is considered to be a man who favours mutual understanding and the peaceful settlement of differences, as well as being an outspoken friend of the Germans. For this reason, and because of his attitude to the conduct of the war, he had not become successor to Archbishop Lang of Canterbury as had been expected. He is said to have visited Germany often and to have been on familiar terms with Rudolf Hess. At the beginning he evidently endeavoured to come to an understanding with the German Evangelical Church under Müller but then turned his attention to the Confessing Church and established connections with Niemöller, Dibelius and Koch.

The purpose of Bishop Bell's visit to Sweden was, according to Bonhoeffer, to enquire into the relations between Sweden and the Soviet Union and study the movements in the Scandinavian Churches. Bell explained that he had spoken at length with Eden before leaving England and had asked him what he should do if peace-feelers were extended from any particular direction in Sweden. Eden had told him quite bluntly that there was no question of England discussing peace terms before it had won the war. In this matter Eden was totally in agreement with Churchill.

The attitude of Sir Stafford Cripps to these problems was quite different from that of Eden. It was quite wrong to say that Sir Stafford was a Bolshevik. It would be more accurate to describe him as a Christian Socialist. Sir Stafford evidently spoke with great concern about the power of Russia, which almost everyone in England underestimated. He had good relations with sources of information in Moscow and feared that no other power, not even England, would be in a position to stop the Russians from advancing as far as the Brandenburg Gate. He thought the consequences of a Russian victory were unforeseeable, as far as England was concerned. Bell had explained that church circles in England were more in agreement with this view of the situation than with Eden's.

When Lord Bishop Bell was asked if the USA would allow England to be destroyed or absorb it into the federation, he replied that this was totally out of the question. America needed a strong bulwark in Europe, and England without its empire would not be strong. On the subject of a possible union between the USA and England Bell did not wish to go into details.

During the course of the interview Bell had commented on the visit which Lord Beaverbrook had evidently recently made to Switzerland. Beaverbrook had had meetings with German industrialists and had discussed with them the possibilities of negotiating peace terms with a view to forming a common front between the Western powers and Germany against Russia. *Dietrich Bonhoeffer* pp. 806–7

Bonhoeffer's last letter to his parents is still asking for books. It was written on 17th January, 1945.

Many have told the story of Bonhoeffer's end. It is known to history now. But none had a better right to tell that story and few could tell it with more real sense of loss than Bishop Bell. He has told the story many times. I have chosen the occasion of a visit to Göttingen in 1957. There in a lecture he retold the whole story of the meeting in Sweden, the arrest, the trial, the failure of the July Plot, and 'the end'. Here are his closing words:

On 9th April, 1945, together with Admiral Canaris and General Oster, he was executed in the concentration camp at Flossenbürg, aged thirty-nine. When he was taken off to the scaffold, he sent me a message through Captain Payne Best, a British fellow-prisoner: 'Tell him', he said, 'that for me this is the end but also the beginning – with him I believe in the principle of our universal Christian brotherhood which rises above all national interests, and that our victory is certain – tell him too that I have never forgotten his words at our last meeting.'

In the same month other members of the Bonhoeffer family met a similar fate. Dietrich's brother Klaus, and his two brothers-in-law, Hans von Dohnanyi and Rüdiger Schleicher, were all murdered.

Hans Schönfeld's sufferings were of a different kind, but they were very deep. He endured great strain, and faced the many dangers to which he was exposed during his journeys from Germany to Geneva with high courage. His health after the war deteriorated greatly, and he fell a victim to a prolonged nervous illness. He died in Frankfurt am Main on 1st September, 1954, at the age of fifty-four.

I know that it is said by some leading British historians and others that the plot of 20th July was doomed to failure, that the Resistance was vacillating, rash and disunited, and that the German generals would never have brought themselves to take decisive action. I know too that in the summer of 1942 the position of the Allies was critical from the military point of view, and that those charged with the direction of the war were absorbed in dealing with military problems. Nevertheless, my own strong conviction is that the negative attitude of the Allies was wrong; that the sound and statesmanlike policy would have been to offer a positive response to the approaches made at such terrible risk; and that the failure to do so was tragic. But the principal point which I want to urge is this. The driving force behind the Resistance movement was a moral force. I do not dispute that there were different elements in it, not all on the same level of moral and religious inspiration. But its leaders were men of high ideals, to whom Hitler and all his works were an abomination. Its finest spirits stood for a Germany purged of totalitarianism and the lust for aggression. It was of the very essence of the Resistance movement that it should aim at the building up of the national, economic and social life, both of Germany and Europe, on the fundamental principles of the Christian faith and life. It is no wonder, surely, that members of the Christian Church in Germany, both Protestants and Catholics, should be prominent in it. Nor should it be surprising that churchmen outside Germany who knew something of the conflict within that country should give it public support, even in time of war. I count it personally a high honour to have been with these two German pastors who came to Sweden in 1942 in the cause of truth, justice and freedom. In the words of Dietrich Bonhoeffer, 'I believe in the principle of our universal Christian brotherhood which rises above all national interests'.

Finally I make bold to claim that, at this juncture in human history, the future of Europe and of the whole world of nations depends on whether or not statesmen and leaders in the different walks of life show the same brave and disinterested loyalty to truth, justice and freedom, in national and international affairs, that the finest spirits of the Resistance Movement in Germany showed during the Second World War.   G.S.I pp. 399–413

Index

Index of Scriptural References

Index of Personal Names

General Index

73 74 75 76 77 10 9 8 7 6 5 4 3 2 1